Lead Generation
Theory and Practice

Ksenia Andreeva

Copyright © 2016 Ksenia Andreeva
All rights reserved.
ISBN-10: 1530771919
ISBN-13: 978-1530771912

CONTENTS

INTRODUCTION 6
Winds of Change in the Marketing Sector 6
   Marketing to Spring Sales.. 6
   What is Included in the Book?.. 7
Based on Practical Experience.. 11
   The Brains Behind the Book.. 11
   The Workings of a Lead Generation Agency 12
   About Me 13
Who Should Read this Book?... 15
   A Must Read for Those on the Fringe with Customers 15
   For Companies Performing Direct Sales 16
PART 1. LEAD GENERATION THEORY 17
What is Lead Generation? 17
   A Wonderfully Effective Marketing Technique 17
   Focusing on Leads 18
   Who Needs Lead Generation? 19
   Not Everyone's Cup of Tea 22
Is Lead Generation Working Like Clockwork for You?............................ 24
   Marketing Business Processes 24
   Lead Generation Corporate Manual.. 26
   Target Audience.. 29
   A General Model of the Lead Generation Workflow 31
   Lead Generation Results in Numbers 37
   Lead Qualification Criteria: Separating the Wheat from the Chaff........ 44
   Lead Nurturing: What Goes Around Comes Around 53
   Sales and Lead Generation: Shaken, Not Stirred..................................... 55
   Budgeting Lead Generation and Lead Cost 57
PART 2. PRACTICE OF LEAD GENERATION 61
Lead Generation Methods... 61
   Overview.. 61
   Good Old Telesales... 65
   Matchmaking: The Key to a Customer 70
   Industry Shows and Hosted Events: Better Alive.................................... 74

- Market Research for Gaining Leads 81
- E-mail Marketing to Encourage Action 83
- Snail Mail for Lead Generation 86
- Mailing Mass Media Subscribers 89
- An Undiscovered Potential of SMS-Marketing 90
- A Corporate Website as a Trap for Leads 92
- Search Engine Advertising 95
- Leads from Social Networks 102
- Ads on Individual Websites and Online Resources to Gain Leads 105
- Print Mass Media and Outdoor Ads, Radio and TV for Lead Generation 107

Marketing Pieces for Lead Generation 109
- Armed by Testing 109
- Landings for Boosting Sales 112
- Call Scripts Bring Leads 118
- Lead Generation Letters 123
- Marketing Lists as a Foundation for Direct Sales 126

Software to Optimize Lead Generation Processes 129
- Innovations to Serve Marketing 129
- Customer Relationship Management (CRM) System 130
- Email Marketing Software 132
- Landing Page Generators 133
- Marketing Automation Software 134
- Knowledge Management 135
- Collaboration and To-Do Lists 136
- Marketing Lists Services 137
- Call Center and IP-Telephony 138
- Shared Calendar Apps 139

PART 3. A LEAD GENERATION TEAM 140
Building a Team 140
- The Myth about "Easy" Marketing and the Reality 140
- Telemarketers 141
- Copywriters and Writers 143
- Contact List Managers 144
- Stick-and-Carrot Tactic for Lead Generation Managers 145

Outsourcing vs Hiring In-House 147
- Leads to Take Away: Pros and Cons 147
- Types of Leads Providers 149
- How much does a lead cost when outsourced? 152

Final Remarks 154
- What if lead generation "does not work?" 154
- Conclusion 156

INTRODUCTION

Winds of Change in the Marketing Sector
Marketing to Spring Sales

Recently, marketing has undergone serious change. Marketers have faced increasing demand to provide quantitative data representative of their work, particularly focusing on **sales growth** in correlation with a narrow target audience. As marketers strive to cultivate new customers directly, they have turned to a growing area of interest: lead generation.

This book has a purely practical purpose, serving as an introductory resource to principles and methods that will enable marketing professionals to raise the number of potential customers and multiply the number of sales typically received. The book will describe and apply the following:

- **lead generation theory**: its basic concepts, and methods of evaluating a return on marketing investments;
- **customer detection techniques**: cold calls, pay per click, mailings, events, etc.;
- **peculiarities and challenges** of lead generation campaigns and methods to overcome obstacles;
- **real stories** about the way companies do lead generation and calculate its results.

The book will not cover the sales process that follows lead generation. Negotiations, persuasion, preparation of business proposals and closing deals are widely covered in other resources. Our focus will cover **marketing tactics that aim to find potential customers**, which allow readers the unique opportunity to engage in lead generation.

At its core, lead generation exists in many enterprises, not just marketing and sales. This fact may surprise readers. In Monsieur Jourdain of Moliere's comedy[1], too, the protagonist was amazed that he had been speaking prose all his life without thinking about the process. But even for those unsurprised readers, few can say with confidence that their company's lead generation is transparent and objective. However, readers will learn that effective lead generation, discussed in this book, is a **transparent business process that brings objective results**. Efficiency in lead generation eliminates the risk that a business will run out of potential customers. Having a steady lead generation process makes it possible to protect a company from periodic dips in sales. Steady lead generation prevents wasting a marketing budget on meaningless activities, which costs a lot of money, but brings little to no result. If one has a well-functioning lead generation process, a company's management knows:

- an optimal cost per finding a prospective customer (lead);
- the amount of time required to find potential customers of various readiness levels to make a purchase;
- which marketing efforts are the most cost-effective;
- how many potential customers are likely to be obtained from a particular activity (e.g., advertising with Google or telemarketing);
- how many of the potential customers will become sales.

With the help of lead generation, a company influences a greater **number of potential customers, analyzes their quality, and ideally takes control to create more sales.** As a result, a company can objectively affect its sales growth and profit. All this – thanks to an effective marketing strategy!

What is Included in the Book?

This book is divided into **three sections.**

The first section highlights **theoretical aspects of lead generation** and communicates how to create an effective process that will serve your goals. The second part reveals **practical steps** to detect potential customers through real-life examples and advice provided by lead generation specialists. While you may be tempted to jump to the second section, the theoretical basis allows you to access a common

---

[1] "Le Bourgeois gentilhomme," - Molière, 1670

understanding about lead generation and attain background knowledge that you will apply to the second section's case studies and tips; this understanding coupled with tips will increase the efficiency of your lead generation process. The third section features **lead generation outsourcing**, which will interest readers who seek to understand the possibility and practicality of outsourcing.

The book also presents the results of a **global benchmark report: "Lead Generation: Strategies and Tactics for 2016."** This survey covered 259 respondents from information and telecommunication technologies, consulting, banking, wholesale, insurance, auto-dealers, etc. The job titles of the respondents are as follows: lead generation directors and managers; chief marketing officers and marketing managers; chief sales officers and managers; chief commercial and business development officers and managers; and owners and managers of subsidiaries. "Lead Generation: Strategies and Tactics for 2016" is the first international analytic report to gather 2015 results and 2016 plans on company lead generation from a wide range of industries. Using this survey, we hope to gain some objectiveness about lead generation processes within enterprises, which is always a kind of privileged information.

Pic. 1. Survey Demographics: Job title category
Source: © NWComm. A Benchmark Report on Lead Generation Strategies and Tactics for 2015-2016

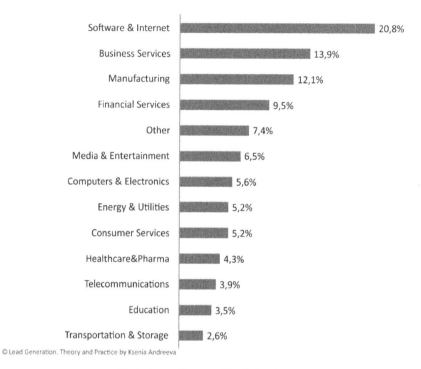

Pic. 2. Survey Demographics: Industries
Source: © NWComm. A Benchmark Report on Lead Generation Strategies and Tactics for 2015-2016

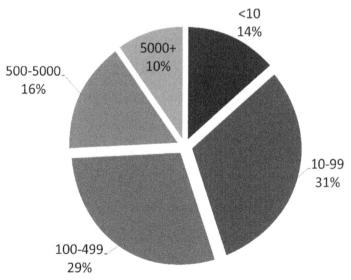

Pic. 3. Survey Demographics: Number of Employees
Source: © NWComm. A Benchmark Report on Lead Generation Strategies and Tactics for 2015-2016

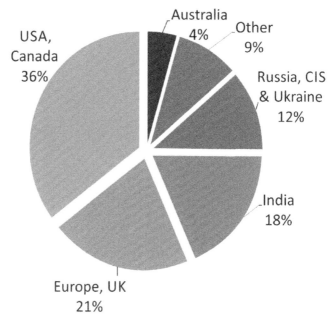

Pic. 4. Survey Demographics: Geography
Source: © NWComm. A Benchmark Report on Lead Generation Strategies and Tactics for 2015-2016

Based on Practical Experience
The Brains Behind the Book

The roots of this book draw on the experience of **NWComm**, a **lead generation agency** (www.nwcomm-marketing.com) that my partners and I run. NWComm focuses on business-to-business lead generation via cold calling for emerging markets. Our business is also concerned with acquiring, selling, and exchanging direct business contacts lists. From 2009-2015, NWComm's team has completed more than 170 lead generation and marketing projects to gain prospective customers and partners for our customers, while simultaneously supporting this process with other marketing tools (e-mail marketing, events, PR). We have searched and found potential customers for our clients in the following spheres:
- information technologies;
- telecommunications;
- corporate education;
- non-profit associations;
- automotive;
- events.

We have customers in the USA, Italy, Holland, Israel, and Russia. Even though there are local specifics in every country (and even in every region), the basic principles described in this book remain the same for each locale. The real experience of enterprises that are included as examples within this book will interest every company that wants to optimize its marketing and sales processes.

The Workings of a Lead Generation Agency

Our team found the idea of providing lead generation services almost intuitively. When we started in 2009, like most businesses doing their first steps in the market, we were ready to do "anything for your money": telemarketing, public relations, events, marketing surveys - and even recruiting.

After less than a half a year since our start, we have realized that 95% of our customers were only truly interested in those activities that helped them to speed up the sales process. At the same time, the majority of our customers did not want to take the plunge and pay for our process (they were not interested in a backstage at all), but highly appreciated our results - **contacts of potential clients who had expressed some interest in their services or products**. Using these contacts, our customers could start doing sales actively. Having evaluated the experience and potential of our team, we realized that we should concentrate on this process as our core area of business.

Our first customers for lead generation with whom we utilized the pay per result principle became, to some extent, our consultants and partners when we developed our own lead generation outsourcing concept and internal business process.

Making cold calls on behalf of our customers to arrange business meetings with prospective clients became one of our primary services. The calls demanded a very high level of attention, as we addressed the C-level of medium and large enterprises. We did not want to sound like a speech synthesis machine, which is the problem of most call centers. Rather, we wanted to sound like business development employees or marketing managers. Using a step-by-step methodology, we expanded our knowledge in customer verticals and expanded our services as we completed new projects and organized professional training.

As a business with firm ethics, our team only worked with **non-competing products**. Choosing competing products would have contradicted our ethical basis; if we had offered similar or even the same products from different suppliers, an internal competition of products would arise, which would be unfair to our customers.

About Me

Before launching my own business, I had worked in senior positions of a business-to-business (B2B) marketing agency and in a company that offered implementations of enterprise management, logistic planning, and financial software. I had experience managing sales, marketing, and lead generation teams, while also coordinating business development, PR, and events.

Most of all, in my work, I loved and still love the **magic of words**. When using proper words (and having relevant proofs for them, of course) a client can move from a categorical "No, never," to "Ok, maybe I'll take a gold sponsorship with two speaking slots with a strong focus on promotion in local mass media." This process is magic, isn't it? In 2009, I felt that a part of my career was coming to a close. I was fueled by my strengths, competences, and a desire to do something of my own. In addition, I had versatile experience that enabled me to handle nearly all business occasions. Drawing from my expertise, NWComm was launched.

While completing our projects, NWComm has acquired the **experience of finding new potential customers for companies of different scales and specializations**. In this book, I want to share my experience. I'll discuss nuances that must be taken into account when doing lead generation and dealing with potential customers. I hope this will help you to make the most of your marketing efforts and find the most cost-effective tactics for your marketing budget. Although my direct experience is only comprised of few industries, the main principles of lead generation are applicable to all companies working in a highly competitive environment and conducting direct sales.

Who Should Read this Book?
A Must Read for Those on the Fringe with Customers

The number of professionals **specializing strictly in lead generation continues to grow each day.** According to the USA's LinkedIn Jobs, as of February 16, 2016, the number of jobs for lead generation managers and directors is only 10 times smaller than all the vacancies related to marketing; quantitatively, this results in 397,769 openings in marketing and 37,590 for openings in lead generation. This book will help professionals keep their skills sharp and to think out of the box as they approach this growing field.

Marketing departments also perform lead generation. However, some marketers find that lead generation is the dullest part of their everyday job, which can result in lead generation being viewed as a necessary evil. As some marketers view lead generation as tedious work, marketing departments may perform the task of finding contacts of potential customers with little enthusiasm. Despite the often unenthusiastic approach, professionals need to realize that **lead generation is a job that is highly appreciated by a company's top management,** as the process creates concrete results that show marketing works.

To gain recognition, appreciation, and concrete results, each marketing specialist must master lead generation techniques. This book will be of great value to:

- lead generation specialists;
- marketing managers, PR, and advertising specialists;
- sales and channels specialists and business development professionals;
- telemarketers and call center operators;

- top management of companies that do direct sales;
- everyone who needs to increase the number of potential customers, and, consequently, sales.

For Companies Performing Direct Sales

The book may interest professionals involved in these **key verticals** of the business-to-business sector:
- distribution and wholesale;
- consulting;
- business services;
- information technologies;
- telecommunications;
- heavy industries;
- banks and financial services for enterprises;
- corporate education.

Lead generation principles are also of great value to companies in the business-to-consumer (B2C) sector:
- insurance companies;
- banks, financial services and credit institutions for end customers;
- real estate services;
- health care;
- education and training;
- automotive;
- travelling and event agencies;
- luxury products and services.

Also, this book will interest suppliers of fast-moving consumer goods, and retailers who seek to establish wholesale sales channels.

PART 1. LEAD GENERATION THEORY

What is Lead Generation?
A Wonderfully Effective Marketing Technique

Lead generation is a **marketing activity aimed at acquiring direct contacts of a seller's prospective customers** that have demonstrated some interest in the seller's goods and services. A potential client found as a result of such an activity is called a **lead**. Lead generation fuels the sales process. Lead generation significantly differs from **brand awareness and PR**. This difference occurs in how each reaches and influences a group of prospective customers. Lead generation's strategy focuses on finding and determining a specific level of interest the individual potential buyers possess, regardless of whether the consumer is a business or a person.

Lead generation is based on **statistics and testing**, which makes the process **more science than art**. It has more techniques and technologies than creativity and inspiration. However, I would not say that a lack of creativity is bad in this process; how could a bad thing be one that brings sales and profit? Lead generation is characterized by clarity of objects and results. It aims to achieve **certain quantitative goals and seeks to gain the maximum return on investment.**

Lead generation provides concrete data and results. For example, the result of participation at an event is not classified as qualitative data such as "Our booth was fantastic" and "We ran out of brochures." Rather, the result is quantitative, indicating that "15 potential customers with a high probability of purchase were found in addition to 50 potential customers with moderate interest, and 15 with a low possibility of purchase." In summation, lead generation **is a marketing tactic that enables a measurement of a marketing activity's efficacy by its sales outcome.**

The following methods we will discuss calculate the return on marketing investments and allow you to estimate how much profit these customers have brought. The methodologies and formulas used to calculate this return, while simple, will be discussed in detail in the next few chapters. With these formulas, marketing costs will **no longer be considered a money pit**. Instead, marketing costs will become **meaningful investments with certain dividends**. This transformation will be evident to your CFO as well!

Focusing on Leads

Different companies, depending on the nature of their business, use the term "lead" with some variation. To some companies, a lead is any incoming request or response to their marketing activity. For example, a "like" of your group on Facebook or a subscription to your newsletter may be considered a lead. Other companies suggest that interested customers can only be treated as leads if the customers have a budget and are ready to buy something in the near future.

In common sense terminology, a **lead** is a potential customer of your target audience who shows a buying interest and has revealed his or her contact information. After having acquired a lead and prior to beginning the sales process, one must check the lead's quality. Quality control for leads is usually based on some criteria, which may be having a need, budget, interest, etc. Lead qualification is one of the most important parts of lead generation and will be discussed more thoroughly in a future chapter.

The respondents of the Benchmark Report on Lead Generation 2015-2016 shared their opinion on the ways **a lead can reveal itself.** Most of the respondents confirm that a lead reveals itself by an incoming call regarding products or services (62%) and an agreement to a business meeting (60%). Less than half of the respondents consider that a request for a call from a sales manager is also a lead revealing characteristic. Among other actions helping to identify a lead are: requests via e-mail, fax, or feedback forms; downloads of white papers, case studies or other company marketing pieces; a positive response to a direct mail; and interest identified as a result of telemarketing. Only 8% of respondents consider a social network activity or a subscription to a newsletter as a lead revealing characteristic.

Pic. 5. How does a lead reveal itself for your company?
Source: © NWComm. A Benchmark Report on Lead Generation Strategies and Tactics for 2015-2016

Who Needs Lead Generation?

Lead generation is necessary for **all the companies with direct sales that need more deals** and want to optimize their sales business processes. These companies mostly target a narrow audience rather than buyers of mass goods like ice-cream, washing machines, and toothpaste. Using lead generation tactics allows these companies to make their marketing activities as efficient as possible. These activities focus on finding potential customers of a certain quality and quantity.

Two main groups of companies truly benefit from lead generation, which results in increased profit. These two groups differ not by size and industry but mostly by specifics of their sales process. The first group includes **companies doing active direct sales and having quite high average profit per each deal**. These enterprises that belong to the first group require lead generation as a separate function to support sales. As a rule, these are business-to-business companies. However, some of the first group may be business-to-customer enterprises such as a wedding agency or a luxury travelling company. In general, these are companies for which:

- Mass advertising and PR do not bring measurable results or do not satisfy their goals.
- The sales process involves personal contact with a potential customer.
- Customers need individual commercial proposals.
- There are sales managers who know how to close deals but they lack time to find new leads.

~~~ *Tip* ~~~
Using brand awareness tactics for products that are sold via personal communication is like using a sledgehammer to crack a nut.
The means must correspond to the end!

Running a smooth lead generation process requires supporters, which here are usually the CEO and sales director. They are interested in providing a steady flow of new potential customers. These potential customers need to be found in advance (sometimes several months before a deal date) to ensure business stability. Marketing managers can also be the initiators of launching a lead generation business process. Thus, they have an opportunity to bring real value and a measurable contribution in sales growth to their company, as well as enhance their image in the eyes of a strict CFO.

The companies that comprise the second group are **mostly in the consumer sector**. These companies do not have lengthy negotiations in their sales process; customers can make a purchase quite quickly individually or will have minimal consultation with a seller. Some examples of these enterprises are car dealers, credit organizations, insurance services, Internet shops, and online resources with a paid subscription. In addition, there are B2B companies that do not use direct sales (e.g., sellers of some types of office equipment and furniture).

These are the companies where:

- The primary function of marketing is to increase sales.
- Brand promotion is a separate goal, requiring its own methodologies.
- The majority of customers do not need individual commercial proposals (or they are very simple).
- The company knows its target audience and understands where to "catch" it.

In such companies, a marketing department is aware of its main goal: attracting new customers. Through the use of lead generation techniques, marketers will acquire real figures for argumentation of their marketing activities and justification of their budget. As a result, the marketing department will be able to increase its value as an efficient business unit and the company will gain profit, enabling an expansion of its market share.

Not Everyone's Cup of Tea

Despite all the advantages of lead generation, there are several groups of companies for which lead generation remains irrelevant. First are **mass market companies**. These companies have a very broad target audience – in fact, everyone. Such companies are well-known around the globe, including Coca-Cola, Wrigley, Bosch, and Lufthansa. They advertise through a variety of media, including television and periodicals. These companies may invite pop stars, organize product placement in movies, and ensure their campaigns are as creative as possible. These companies have a huge advertising budget but can only calculate an approximation of its effectiveness. In short, these are the businesses that epitomize John Wanamaker's words[2]: "Half of our

---

[2] John Wanamaker (July 11, 1838 – December 12, 1922) - a United States' merchant, religious leader, civic, and political figure, that some consider to be a proponent of advertising and a "pioneer

advertising budget is wasted, only we do not know what it is."

In the business-to-business sector, there are also companies that do not need new clients. Such companies do not need new clients due to a narrowness of market or due to insufficient resources. These companies have **anchor customers** through long-term relationships. For example, a provider of telecommunication services in a particular office building is unable to sell more of its services than there are renters (although, of course, such providers can periodically upsell additional services).

Moreover, in most countries, new leads are not needed in **governmental bodies** and those who serve them, as well as those in the public sector, housing and utilities, non-commercial education, and healthcare. For many regions, these bodies have no competitors, and thus, have no need to fight for their customers. (The issue of governmental loyalty is another topic that, while very important, is outside our scope.)

Monopolies also do not have a critical need for lead generation because they already occupy a major market niche. However, these companies can actively promote their service category. For example, the city railway station may attract new customers by focusing on the convenience of trains compared to other means of transportation, such as being faster than foot, cheaper than cars, and safer than aircraft. In addition, monopolies may have to market new products, which results in a struggle for buyers' attention.

Lead generation (at least in its full extent) is not a must for companies conducting **fewer than 10-20 sales per year**. In these cases, the sales function is usually centralized and can be performed by even top management. I know a CEO of a large consulting company who performs cold calling and lead nurturing himself. "There's never a second chance to make a first impression," he said. In this particular case, his approach produced great results. The target market was narrow and all the deals were very large, which enabled the process to be handled by one person.

In general, trying to build a stable business independent from the human factor in a highly competitive business environment is impossible without lead generation. Without lead generation, your process is a risky mechanism where income depends on random factors. As a result, companies often try to increase sales volume by **hiring another sales manager**. Perhaps hiring another manager will help, but that action remains a gamble. If another sales manager is acquired and sales do not increase, lead generation tactics should be instated. Let's discuss in the

---

in marketing." Source: Wikipedia

next chapter how lead generation can be implemented.

Is Lead Generation Working Like Clockwork for You?
Marketing Business Processes

A business process is a **set of corresponding tasks** that culminate in the delivery of a service or product. A business process can also be defined as a set of activities and tasks that, once completed, will accomplish an organizational goal. This process is constantly reproduced and, therefore, is predictable, which is its primary difference from a process that is only repeated once. An example of a one-time process is the creation of a slogan for a new product, which is completed through a single action and cannot be described as a business process (unless you work for a creative agency that specializes in slogan creation). On the other hand, an example of a business process may be the organization of roadshows for customers; this process will always include the following tasks: booking a venue, inviting guest speakers, gathering delegates, reminding them about the event, and conducting follow-up calls. These processes can be described in a chart: if action A is done positively, then B, if negatively, then C. If you are in D with X results, do Z. Have you done Z? Congratulations, you are in Y – reaching the end and completing the process!

Following a business process **eliminates a need for creativity** in most common operations. Readers may wonder why I do not like creativity. The answer is – I love creativity! However, a job must be completed, regardless of one's inspiration. The work has to be done with certain qualitative and quantitative results and should be performed regularly. This work should also be predictive, and creativity means risks, which is a gamble that we are unable to afford. We are not playing in a casino. All companies need to pay salaries and have regular costs. Therefore, it is necessary that all business processes should **work like clockwork,** or, at minimum, tend to do so.

In addition, a business process should include the **generalized knowledge of more experienced colleagues**. Following a business process is especially important for new employees, as it enables them to quickly get into the flow of things and start working with maximum efficiency, which is exactly what the head of a department wants to see, without having to deal with the same questions from employees over and over again.

Bill Gates once said: "Virtually every company will be going out and empowering their workers with a certain set of tools, and the big difference in how much value is received from that will be how much the company steps back and really thinks through their business processes, thinking through how their business can change, how their project management, their customer feedback, their planning cycles can be quite different than they ever were before." These words also apply to marketing business processes, as now there comes the time to make their routine as predictive and automated as possible.

Successful companies always **optimize their business processes to reach business expansion and scalability**. They invest considerable resources in improving production, logistics, finance, procurement and sales. This helps limit the cost of performing routine procedures, increases the effectiveness of information exchange, and reduces errors. Similar advantages are achieved by optimization of marketing activities, primarily, lead generation. This involves a description of tasks, including listing basic steps, forming a sequence of action, drafting outcome options and analyzing results. You can use different methods such as verbal description, drawing flowcharts, outlining business processes in software (e.g., Customer Relations Management), and regular staff training. Each company chooses its own tools and methods. The primary aim is process transparency and predictability.

Learning to stop at the right moment when describing a business process is crucial. The practical value of information decreases if people take too long to digest and learn it. If you have to study something for too long, the information becomes useless, since you have no time to implement it. And, second, the information may become outdated before you have learned it, if there is too much of it. I would take my advice and move on to the next chapter.

Lead Generation Corporate Manual

Do you love Starbucks? I love their spiced tea latte. And I especially love the words of their CEO Howard Schultz, who declared: "People want guidance, not rhetoric; they need to know what the plan of action is and how it will be implemented. They want to be given responsibility to help solve the problem and the authority to act on it."

To begin, there are several types of **corporate manuals** that describe how companies work, the requirements of business processes, and the most effective techniques. Many companies have brand books regulating the use of their corporate identity and sales books describing their sales process. It is useful to create a **guide that describes the process of lead generation** either within a sales book or a separate manual. The process of finding customers for your business is unique and this is a task that you know better than anyone else. It is important to share this knowledge with co-workers or an outsourcing agency (which may be changed and needs to be brought on board as quickly as possible) as you tackle a common goal. Creation of a corporate lead generation manual will save you time and nerves, as you will no longer be subjected to repeat presentations on the main principles of lead generation and will no longer face a variety of interpretations on the subject. After agreeing on documentation with all concerned departments – marketing, sales, commercial and financial departments, plus top managers – you will avoid misunderstanding the main issues.

The **lead generation manual** usually covers the following topics:

- basic products and services for lead generation and their marketing positions;
- key benefits of paying attention during initial contact with prospective customers;
- analysis of competitors, your competitive advantages;
- objections handling;
- target audience criteria and description of their motivation to purchase;
- basic principles that must be followed in marketing materials: letters, call scripts, landings, etc.;
- software guides such as work in CRM;
- target quantitative and qualitative criteria;
- lead qualification process;
- lead generation budget;
- cadence and touching points;
- lead nurturing;

- planning and reporting scheme;
- anything else you feel is important to include, which will help your colleagues to understand the process and follow a corporate standard.

If the decision-making process of your customer is a long story and includes many personal communications, such as business meetings and phone calls, **do not break down the communication cycle and include in a lead generation manual all aspects of sales**. This is a different science (despite having much in common). Of course, lead generation managers should know the main sales principles and be able to convince customers to purchase. However, their specialty must be to find and identify as many leads as possible. Further communication should be handed to sales managers, who master the techniques of closing sales and know the features of products and their pricing.

Here is an **example** of how one of our partner companies working in IT **has launched a new lead generation and sales process**. This is a B2B company doing direct sales with a long purchase cycle. Its managing partner said: "Previously we had been looking for customers in the Internet and Yellow Pages, making cold calls, and saying something like 'Do you need our software?' Then, our sellers had been tormenting those who responded with something like 'Ok, maybe, call back in a month.' This approach provided some results but overall had been unstable and unpredictable. This unreliability is not what we had wanted to see.

Due to these unfavorable results, we **fired all the sales managers**. Everyone! Then, we sat down and determined our **target audience**. We identified several target groups and the features of prospective customers. Then, for each target group, we drafted a list of criteria by which they chose their suppliers. Through this research, we first understood how to interact with these prospects and how to nurture them in the future. For some of them, we provided valuable content and thus demonstrated our professionalism; for others, we suggested seminars and webinars. Depending on the potential customer, we appealed to personal recommendations given by existing clientele.

We did not try making speed sales. Firstly, we offered something useful such as white papers, events, and free consulting. We even sometimes refused those customers, who, in our view, had no need of our software. We only **started a sales process** when a lead became nurtured enough to ask the price. If a client needed additional time to think about a purchase, we transferred that person back to the nurturing stage, where we again provided valuable content and made personal contact from time to time.

We developed our own system to qualify potential customers and made our own rules detailing how to contact them. These actions allow our 'expensive' sales managers not to waste time on irrelevant presentations and unnecessary calls. As a result, we now **actively work only warm leads** with incoming requests. Our profit has increased in comparison to our previous strategy of having the sales department conduct cold calls.

Our experience shows that the following is the best lead generation strategy:

- the marketing department seeks new contacts;
- the telesales managers identify new leads;
- the sales managers work with contacts on their level and close deals.

As we deal with a larger number of contacts, we use **CRM**, which enables us to reduce our time through functions that process the information for us and eliminate the risk of forgetting about taking action during customer correspondence. The system's analytics is of great value as well. We find the **e-mail marketing** function also useful; it allows us not just to send out e-mails but also to get feedback and an analysis of addressees that have opened, read, and followed a link in the letter. This makes the initial step of finding prospects with whom we can progress to the next level easier."

Target Audience

It is said that if a company does not break the market into segments, then it is the market that will break the company into segments. So let's talk about market segmentation. Market segmentation is created through a **definition of target groups.** A target group in lead generation usually refers to a group of potential customers that have common characteristics. For **B2C companies**, the target audience can be determined by the following basic criteria:
- geography (residence and employment);
- demographics (gender, age, income, occupation, marital status, etc.);
- psychology (personality type, lifestyle, interests, and personal values);
- behavior (possession of objects, request for certain information, any actions taken).

For the B2B sector, the criteria that determine the target audience are as follows:
- geography (headquarters and branch offices);
- governmental/corporate (or B2B)/consumer (or B2C) sector;
- industry/vertical;
- company size (by revenue, number of employees);
- job title of a decision maker;
- any additional criteria which are specific to a particular product.

The key to successful lead generation is correctly defining customer target groups and their motivation for buying. To understand your target audience, conducting **marketing research** is a must. Such research will verify assumptions about the interests of potential buyers and validate your promotion strategy. Target group research is particularly important when bringing innovative products to market. Otherwise, the professionals involved in lead generation may lose time and money on useless activities and even worse: **they waste the time of sales managers**. This may damage business, as for many modern enterprises, the company's employees' time is very closely related to company profit.

Understanding your target audience will help you choose the **right marketing instruments and advertising space**. This is especially important for manufacturers of **consumer goods**, since they work with broad customer groups, and, in most cases, cannot possess the personal information of prospective customers. Yes, you can address them in person via social networks or mass media e-mail newsletters, but this is only for the time of your marketing campaign. You cannot access these lists just anytime for any marketing tactic you want.

Knowing your target audience prompts obvious solutions when choosing advertising space. For example, a seller of extreme tourism advertises in men's magazines. That is clear. However, there may be **striking decisions,** at least at first glance. For example, a manufacturer of network equipment sponsors a beekeeping fair. The products are affordable and the target audience is wide enough: small business. This small business participates in such an exotic event. At the same time, at this show there are no competitors of our smart vendor; its participants are positive and open to the perception of new information. In short, that's a great opportunity to make sales at one's profit.

The basic information about a target audience of **B2B companies** is mainly available from open sources such as the Internet, mass media, and Yellow Pages. You can also purchase a marketing list containing direct contacts of your target audience, and thus, do not spend time on their finding. I shall speak about list providers in detail in one of the next chapters.

Additional criteria for B2B companies in most cases vary for different products. Most of the information about them cannot be found in open sources and they should be explored through direct contacts. For example, a data storage optimization software vendor is worried about the size of an enterprise database; a collaboration system provider pays attention to the number of branch offices.

Sometimes, companies take into consideration rather **subjective characteristics,** such as the spirit of innovation, interest in new technologies, or rational perception of benefits. Well, if you gain deep insight into the business of your potential customer so that you can recognize these things – perfect! However, if you want a steady flow of leads, it is better to follow more objective criteria.

Sometimes, a company **does not know its target audience**, which means it cannot understand who would buy its products or services. This shows that the company does not understand its client. This happens mostly for products that are new to the market. In this case, it is likely that not only lead generation may be difficult, but further sales as well. For example, we tried to collaborate with a startup company for which the main criterion of a target audience was the following: "The main thing about our customers is that they should be willing to buy our services! It does not matter who it is." It is evident that such statement of purpose is fatal in terms of lead generation. In this case, conducting any marketing activity would be like groping in the dark. I think it is similar to the conversation of Alice and the Cheshire Cat:

"Would you tell me, please, which way I ought to go from here?"

"That depends a good deal on where you want to get to," said the Cat.

"I don't much care where" said Alice.

"Then it doesn't matter which way you go," said the Cat.

And last but not least about the target audience theory: sometimes there are companies that are, at first glance, not of your target audience, yet they have their **own reasons for purchasing your product**. For example, implementation of a large-scale IT system is mostly inappropriate for small companies. But it may happen that a large holding acquires a certain small company and this is the reason the company needs to implement the holding's standard system. So, perhaps this is also a lead. In general, do not brush off the possibility of selling to such a business before thoroughly investigating the issue.

A General Model of the Lead Generation Workflow

The **general strategy of lead generation workflow** is shown in Pic.6. First, you need to determine a target audience for the products promoted. At this stage, you should estimate things that pertain to your campaign, such as the demography of online mass media subscribers, the number of visitors at a show, or behaviors such as a search for specific information on Google. Then, you determine an advertising space where you can bring your message to your target audience and prepare marketing materials, which depends on the activity you have chosen. These materials may include content to attract prospective customers, advertisements, landings, e-mail newsletters, a booth, and give-outs for events. For some activities, you will need a list of contacts[3] that you call or send e-mails to – these contacts are called **suspects**.

Then, a **marketing activity** is conducted. Activities include participation in a conference, a telemarketing campaign, pay per click advertising in a search engine or in a social network. At first, you should **test a marketing activity** on a small sample of your suspects or target audience so that you know its efficacy.

As a result of your activity, you will attain a certain number of responses. Among them, there will be positive, neutral and negative responses. These are not leads yet! These responders are usually called **prospects**. Among the prospects, there might be those who are interested in some information for self-education or research. They may actually belong in your non-target group: your partners, journalists, or job seekers. So, you need to check the quality of a prospect. Improper prospects need to be swept aside. Information about them will help you understand how to improve positioning of your product, and, possibly, to modify marketing materials. The usual criteria which allow you to estimate the purchase possibility include evaluation of a prospect's interest, need, budget and purchase planned timeframe (for B2B - authority role as well). This process is called **marketing qualification** and it serves to separate the wheat from the chaff.

The remaining positive suspects answering qualification criteria are called **marketing qualified leads**, which distinguishes them from those that pass the next level of quality control: **sales qualification**. This is done to confirm the information that was found by the marketing department from a sales perspective and takes into account any additional factors that may influence further dealing with this lead. Ideally, a number of marketing and sales qualified leads must coincide. If a sales department rejects lots of leads, you most likely need to correct your marketing qualification criteria or to add a new criterion. Of course, sometimes it happens that the criteria are correct, but a sales department determines, through reasons of its own, why a client has no potential.

---

[3] Do not forget to check on the country's policy regarding calling and sending letters to new addressee. For example, in the USA, there is a National Do Not Call List that is used by all call centers to avoid negative reaction from those who do not want to receive new calls. In some countries, you are not allowed to send mass e-mails to new addressees unless he or she has given you permission to do this (like filled in an application for a discount card and put a check mark to agree to receive information from you).

This instance should be treated as an exception for which everyone should be ready. When sales qualification is finished, we have a fully **qualified lead**.

As a result of lead qualification, you will get **leads with different possibilities of purchasing**. Some of these leads do not have money, but have interest; others have money but are not interested at all. These are usually termed **cold leads** in contrast to warm and hot ones. **Warm and hot leads** are those with a strong possibility of purchasing – these are the customers with the most potential and they should be worked over in the first turn. Closing a deal with these potential customers is called **opportunity.** Cold leads should go to a phase of **nurturing**. Lead nurturing is a set of consequent interactions that warms up leads until they are ready to consider buying. We shall talk about this topic in detail in one of the next chapters.

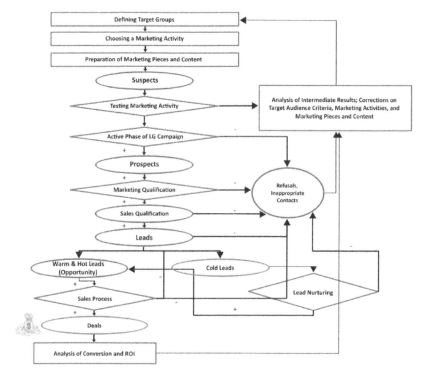

Pic. 6. Lead Generation Workflow.
Here – "+" means a result or an action that moves a purchase process forward; "-" means a result or an action that delays a purchase, or refuses)

The **number of qualified leads** depends on three main factors: a right target audience, a right advertising space or marketing method, and a right message brought to the target group. Lead criteria definitely influence this number: if they are very strict, you will have few leads but those leads will be considered better qualified. If they are somehow flexible, you will get more leads but the majority of these leads will go into nurturing. While conducting your first marketing activity, you cannot predict the output. However, after several similar lead generation activities for the same target audience, you will finally get some average statistics on what to expect and find an ideal balance for your qualification criteria.

~~~ Tip ~~~
- The number of qualified leads depends on:
- target audience;
- marketing channel;
- marketing message;
- content;
- lead qualification criteria;
- demand for your category of goods;
- competitive environment.

What should **micro businesses with a small staff** do where the same people who conduct marketing and sales and sometimes even general management need lead generation? Lead qualification will be even easier for them because there is no other person or department involved in this process. But a general understanding of the principles described above will be useful for them anyway. This will help them set priorities with potential clients that they can address first of all. The time of a manager who performs many functions is extremely valuable. So it is important to work with the customers with the most potential in the first turn.

The general lead generation workflow **does not always come exactly as described above**. It differs for every business due to each individual company's goals, corporate style, technical landscape, and dozens of other factors. These procedures are not always formal, nor do they necessarily have both quality control levels. It is neither good nor bad. Determining efficacy depends on the results. If your lead generation process brings you results that suit you – please do not change anything. However, if you feel that your target market has more potential for you – pay attention to the processes and methods described here in this book. My experience shows that the more detailed the approach is, the more leads a company is able to acquire. Those who need thousands of leads per month pay great attention to marketing qualification and make it as tuned to sales qualification as possible. They try to automate every step of their workflow. On the contrary, a business that needs just a dozen leads per month usually deals with their qualification intuitively. And I absolutely do not insist on complicating the process you have. Make it as simple as you can but scrupulous enough to serve your goals.

Let's illustrate our theory with a **business example** to see how this process works in real life. BrandMaker is a provider of Marketing Resource Management (MRM) systems. The company develops and markets sophisticated software solutions for the marketing communication of medium and large-scale organizations. The company focuses on large and medium enterprises of the B2B sector, particularly those in the financial and manufacturing industries. The titles of these decision makers are C-level marketing, sales, business development, and commercial executives.

Experienced with the best know-how about MRM systems, the company has established a steady and strong lead generation process. The first step in the process of bringing leads to revenue is to receive the contacts of those who are interested in the company's solutions and MRM in general. These contacts are called marketing generated leads. These leads are received via various marketing methods: ads in search engines and relevant websites, LinkedIn, SEO, SEM, blogs, etc. While running these campaigns, the company uses a set of landing pages and constantly practices A/B testings.

Further, the leads need to be qualified from both marketing and sales perspectives. The conversion of marketing generated leads to marketing qualified ones is approximately 33-34%, and from marketing qualified to sales qualified – 35-36%.

Having passed these qualifications, a lead becomes an opportunity and active sales begin. In an equation, the formula is as follows: Marketing Generated Leads => Marketing Qualified Leads => Sales Qualified Leads => Opportunity => Opportunity Management => Closing.

Here are the quantitative results the company has achieved within a year:

Parameter	Result
Marketing Generated Leads (MGL)	1700
Marketing Qualified Leads (MQL)	550
Sales Qualified Leads (SQL)	~200
Cost per Lead	26,50 to 325,00€

Conversion of Qualified Leads to Sales	8-10%

Timm Brocks, **Director Sales Lead Generation for BrandMaker, says:** "Lead generation is one of the core processes within our business, so we dedicate many resources into leveraging a maximum and keeping it within our enterprise. One of my key goals is to develop modern lead generation strategies using social media, online promotion, calls and cadence, touch points, and development of lists segmented by sales channel, customer type, and customer demographics."[4]

Here is another example, describing the lead generation workflow of a marketing agency providing advertising in malls and shopping centers. This agency's CEO said: "The first level of work with new customers is a **call center**. Its main goal is to update contacts lists. The lists are mostly acquired from business information providers, event organizers, etc. Telemarketers of the call center are making first contact by phone. They have call scripts that are specially developed for establishing first contact and they identify basic information about a potential of a suspect. The call center works out 100% of the incoming contacts.

After figuring out the list and obtaining basic information about sales possibility, all the prospects go to a **marketing department** for qualification. This makes it possible to prioritize attention on customers that have the highest possibility of purchasing. I must highlight that, for us, it is important to set priorities, as we have different target groups.

Further, these contacts go to a **presales department**. That is the next stage. Presale managers start to work with selected potential customers to see which of them can go to the next stage – **direct sales**. All the leads are divided between sales managers according to their product competence and target audience specialization. Our approach is that our experts are narrow specialists in their field. They are not aware about every product and service we sell. The further sales work is quite common – managers negotiate with customers, go to business meetings, make commercial proposals, discuss the price, etc. By the way, during this process, they also bring a lot of valuable information about our competitors to the proverbial table.

Step by step, we are making every stage as automated and regulated as possible. Thus, the workflow runs with minimum stops and breakdowns. This mechanism allows us to have a nonstop sales cycle, resulting in making profit."

---

[4] BrandMaker provided this case study. www.brandmaker.com

Lead Generation Results in Numbers

So, how do you get the numbers that allow an estimation of the results from a lead generation campaign objectively? Our **starting point is the number of suspects** from a marketing activity. This may be the number of e-mail recipients or the number of contacts in a list for telemarketing or the number of requests in search engines for your kind of goods, etc.

Then, we look at the **number of prospects** obtained from these suspects as a result of a marketing activity. The prospects may reveal themselves by a positive response to a newsletter, a declaration of some interest in a telephone conversation, or a download of content from a website. When the number of suspects meets your potential customer criteria from a marketing and sales perspective (for example, they have interest, need, budget, etc.), they become **leads.** The percentage of suspects to prospects and of prospects to leads is another factor that is important to take into account when testing various marketing activities.

In different companies, the definition of "suspect" and "prospect" may vary and this is absolutely fine. **Different businesses have different criteria of client potential**. There is no strict dividing line between suspect and prospect. It is also totally up to each business to decide when a prospect "ends" and a lead "starts." For example, for one specialized vendor of CAD/CAM systems, a request for a demo version is the start of the sales cycle, and all persons who have asked for this are treated as leads. At the same time, an online job listing service does not consider those who use their free version as leads because too many people continue working only in free mode and are just prospects.

The proportion between suspects, prospects, and leads brings us to a key notion of lead generation – **conversion**. According to the benchmark report "Lead Generation Strategy and Tactics for 2015-2016," a conversion is the most important criterion when estimating the results of a marketing campaign.

Pic. 7. Which criteria are important for you to estimate
the results of a lead generation campaign?
Source: © NWComm. A benchmark report on Lead Generation Strategy and Tactics for 2015-2016

Conversion is a general term used to describe the ratio of actions performed in respect to one set of objects and in respect to another[5]. It sounds a bit abstract, but it will be more evident when I give examples. In marketing, the word "conversion" is used in two cases. The first is purely concerned with lead generation and sales and does not depend on what marketing instrument is used. This is **the percentage of leads becoming sales, which is the number of sales over the total number of leads**[6]. So this is a ratio of actual and potential customers. For example, if one of 10 leads has agreed to buy a product, then there is a conversion rate of 10%.

$$\text{Conversion (in lead generation)} = \text{Number of sales/number of leads}$$

Second, in **pay per click advertising**, the conversion rate is the

---

[5]According to the Merriam-Webster dictionary: Conversion: 1. the act or process of changing from one form, state, etc., to another. 2. The act or process of changing from one religion, belief, political party, etc., to another.
http://www.merriam-webster.com/dictionary/conversion
[6] This definition is used, for example, in the book Maximizing Lead Generation: The Complete Guide for B2B Marketers by Ruth P. Stevens (Que Publishing, 2011): Conversion: when a lead becomes a sale.
http://www.amazon.com/Maximizing-Lead-Generation-Complete-Marketers/dp/0789741148

ratio of the number of visitors who have done any targeted action on a web page over the total number of visitors who have visited a web page. Targeted actions may include: submitting a form, calling the phone number indicated on a landing page, subscribing to a newsletter, downloading a file, and finally making an online purchase. For example, during a pay per click campaign in Google, a web page was visited by 1,000 people and 200 of them filled out an application form. Hence, the conversion is 200/1000 = 20%.

$$\text{Conversion (in pay per click advertising)} = \text{Number of leads/number of clicks}$$

In this book, I shall use the term "conversion" in its first definition, the one related to sales. So the conversion rate depends on many things. First, conversion depends on **the number of leads and their quality**. That is the correct choice of a target audience, proper marketing channel, relevant content, and adequate lead criteria. But **further sales actions** are also very important.

~~~ *Tip* ~~~
Sales conversion is influenced by:
-lead quality;
-lead quantity;
-sales work;
-competitiveness of your offer;
-market situation.
~~~

Sometimes, it happens that in the same situation, one sales manager is able to sell something, but another quits empty-handed. This occurrence is described in a good old joke. Two shoe sales managers went to Africa to open up new market. A few days later they wrote a report to the headquarters of their companies. The first manager said: "The idea has no effect: in this region there is no target audience – no one wears shoes. I am going back." At the same time, the other salesperson reported: "Awesome place! The prospects are unlimited! Nobody wears shoes here! Immediately send me ten thousand pairs!"

Conversion is also affected by the **competitiveness of your offer, its price, and market situation**. Marketers cannot work wonders if your competitors are aggressively offering the same thing, but cheaper and faster.

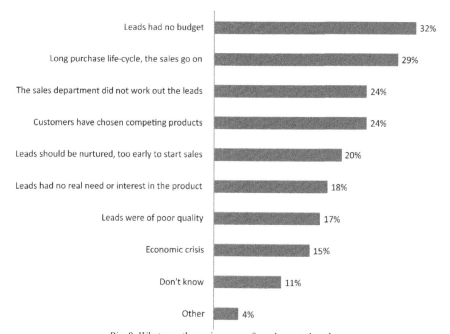

Pic. 8. What was the main reason for sales not closed or customers' delayed decisions in 2015?
Source: © NWComm. A benchmark report on Lead Generation Strategy and Tactics for 2015-2016

Let's go back to sales. The number of leads is often not as important as profit from them (however the number of leads is easier to calculate). The **return on investment (ROI)** is a measure used to assess the effectiveness of an investment or to compare different types of investments[7], and it is used in marketing as well. ROI helps to determine the most effective marketing steps. This method allows you to compare the results of different activities such as participation in exhibitions and direct mail, pay per click advertising and cold calling. At first glance, these activities are incommensurable.

There are many **formulas for calculating ROI**. Different companies use those which better suit their goals. Some formulas can be quite complicated, including various taxes, cost of depreciation, and interest on loans. For this book, we shall use the following formula of ROI in marketing, which is the simplest:

ROI = (Cost of goods sold[8] – marketing expenses)/

---

[7] According to Investopedia, the return on investments (ROI) is a performance measure used to evaluate the efficiency of an investment or to compare the efficiency of a number of different investments.
http://www.investopedia.com/terms/r/returnoninvestment.asp

marketing expenses

Sometimes, ROI can also be estimated in percentages; then the formula's result is multiplied by 100%. This approach is just as applicable, but I prefer simple coefficients without percentages because it makes the numbers shorter.

Here is an example. A foreign language education center uses pay per click advertising on Google. They have completed a set of advertisements and finally have decided to test two samples, to see which has the potential to be the most effective:

Ad#1
Spanish with natives
www.myabcdeschool.com
30% discounts.
Professors from Spain and Catalonia

Ad#2
Spanish education and certification
www.myabcdeschool.com
30% discounts.
CELU, DELE exams

The ads led to different landing pages. Both of them encouraged visitors to immediately fill out a form to get a discount. Prices for two different pages were $499 and $599 per course. Oh, yes, and each landing page gave different phone numbers that allowed tracking on those who preferred calling to filling out forms. Later, we shall speak in detail about the creation of landings and their essential elements.

The cost of one click was approximately $0.5 for the region selected. The total set-up cost of the campaigns was $300. A week after the campaigns' launch, the first advertisement gathered 400 clicks and the second one – 250. 30 people who had clicked on the first ad and 20 people who clicked on the second one filled out a contact form to secure the discount and their seat in a group. They were classified as prospects. Then, a lead generation manager of the center called everyone who had filled out the contact form and invited them to come to their office to

---

[8] According to Investopedia, cost of goods sold (COGS) are the direct costs attributed to the production of goods sold by a company. This amount includes the cost of materials used in creating the good along with the direct labor costs used to produce the good. It excludes indirect expenses such as distribution costs and sales force costs.
http://www.investopedia.com/terms/c/cogs.asp

pass an introduction test and then register for the course. Five of these suspects were disqualified, for example, they had mixed Spanish with Italian, or lived in another city. Things do happen. The rest of the suspects qualified as leads and they were expected to sign a contract and pay. However, a few of them refused for different reasons. For example, someone wanted more of a discount and another had decided to go to Valencia and to study Spanish on site. As a result, the 20 people attracted by the first ad, and the 15 people attracted by the second one signed a contract for training and made a payment. The COGS of each sale are estimated at $300 and $330 respectively for teacher salaries, room rent, training books, etc. Let's calculate what we have as a result:

Parameter	Ad #1 (about Natives)	Ad #2 (about Certifications)
Clicks	400	250
Suspects	30	20
Leads	27	18
Sales	20	15
Conversion	20/27 = 74%	15/18 = 83%
Price of 1 training course	$499	$599
Income	$9980	$10183
COGs for 1 training course	$300	$330
COGs total	$6000	$5610
Pay per click expenses	400 x 0.5 = $200	$250 x 0.5 = $125
Setting up an ads campaign	$180	$120
Total marketing expenses	= $200 + $180 = $380	= $125 + $120 = $245
ROI	14.8	19.5

Let me give another example as an illustration of ROI estimation for **B2B market**. One of our customers provided **information security services**. The company was developing a new business direction and was carefully monitoring the effectiveness of various marketing investments. The director of a new branch division told us that the initiatives proposed by their marketing department included brand participation in events and advertising. Costs for these activities were high and the amount of time wasted was significant; at the same time, no effect was observed. Of course, they influenced their potential customers through brand awareness; however, it was impossible to measure to what extent these customers were influenced. The sales department of the new branch division was unhappy with this direction and took the lead generation process under its own control, subsequently outsourcing it.

Ten months later, they got the following results; more than 100 meetings and conference calls were arranged, and 10 contracts were signed. Another 10 contracts had progressed to the stage of signing and approval. The average cost of a sale was $60,000 while the price per lead was $220-335. The conversion rate of leads into sales was 20% and the return on investment – 36.5%.

Parameter	Business Meetings for Information Security Company
Leads	100 companies
Sales	20
Conversion	20/100 = 20%
Profit / 1 average sale	$52,000
Total Profit	$1,040,000
Cost-per-lead (Average)	$277.5
Marketing Expenses	~277.5 x 100 = $27,750
ROI	(1,040,000 – 27,750)/ 27,750 = 36.5

For many businesses, there are also long-term opportunities that can change the return on investment estimation. These are **long-term customers** who buy from you constantly. It is absolutely up to each business how to take this type of customer into account when calculating a profit from them. For example, you can take the projected profit for the year. To develop a common position on such customers and to use it constantly is crucial.

Now you know how to estimate the effectiveness of various marketing activities and you can adjust these tools to suit your business goals. You can evaluate the quality of different lead generation methods and their variations for your business.

The only remark that remains to be made before making a conclusion about the effectiveness of a marketing activity is to please conduct **several tests**. Yes, tests take time and cost money. However, if you do not conduct them, you run the risk of declining a profitable lead generation method. If you practice a new campaign type for the first time – the conversion rate may be low. The reason of this might be not the method behind the practice, but the correctness of its use.

It also may happen that the conversion rate is **extremely high for the first time** of a marketing activity and this may mislead companies regarding future sales. They begin to wait for high results all the time. For example, we at NWComm did a lead generation campaign by completing cold calls for our customer offering Microsoft solutions for business. During the first month, the conversion was 100% – all the leads signed a contact! That was fantastic! Of course, our customer was happy. But the reason for success was quite simple: we had new marketing methods for a new contact list. We made the right calls to the right people, strictly to the target audience. Further figures aligned with the expected level of 20-30%. However, for this type of product, it was still a very good conversion. Our customer, fortunately, understood this and was ready for such numbers.

Our conclusion holds one more important point. To be aware of the average conversion is extremely important, as it allows you **to plan the workload of lead generation, marketing and sales managers**. You roughly know how many actions you need to perform in order to achieve your goal. For example, you determine how many calls need to be done to find a lead. In this case every refusal becomes valuable and has intrinsic value, as it statistically moves you toward a lead or a sale. This fact always fills me with optimism. Refusals in lead generation are inevitable. It is important to know that if you continue to work, then success and profit will surely come – again, according to statistics.

Lead Qualification Criteria: Separating the Wheat from the Chaff

Lead qualification criteria are characteristics that help to classify a lead by the degree of its willingness and readiness to buy. As a result of this qualification, one can distinguish, in terms of making a purchase, the leads with the most and least potential: hot, warm, and cold.

While determining the criteria for your target audience, please be aware of one important thing: there is always a **balance between the desired quantity and quality of contacts you want to get**. You can use more strict criteria for leads and have fewer of them, which enables you to focus on highly prospective customers. Or you can take broader criteria and thus increase their number, as well as sales work. But perhaps, as a result of your efforts, cold opportunities will warm up faster. Finding a balance between the desired number of leads and their appropriate quality is a matter of testing, correction, and testing again.

In lead generation, these following **five key criteria** that enable an evaluation of a lead's potential are the most common:
- need;
- interest;
- budget;
- timing;
- decision maker's role.

The last two criteria are mainly relevant for corporate sales and products with high value. For consumer good sales, it is sufficient to identify a need, interest, and money. This model of five criteria is similar to the famous **BANT** approach invented by IBM:
- Budget (do they have enough money to buy the product?);
- Authority (can they make a purchase decision?);
- Need (do they have a need that the product or service in question can fulfill?);
- Timescale (do they have a specific time when they wish to make their purchase?).

Lately, there have been lots of critics of the BANT criteria, as the critics see the criteria as too rigid when they are taken literally. "BANT is dead!" they cry. I do not think so. BANT should be utilized philosophically, as a concept rather than rigid practice. Its realization should be adapted to today's reality, when almost every customer can find information before speaking to a salesperson. Another feature that should prevent you from taking BANT literally is that today there are so many innovative products that buyers do not always understand what they need best of all. However, many companies still use BANT as the most simple and common way to rate a lead as cold, warm or hot. So we **revise the BANT criteria**, making them more flexible, and oversee the exceptions.

The need for a certain product or service is the main criterion of qualification. Roughly speaking, either there is a need for a product or not. In one case, a person knows exactly what he or she wants, how many and its specifications. In another case, a need exists but is rather vague. It is interesting that clients may not be aware they have a need. For example, a girl comes to buy her first car and she does not know which additional options she needs. If a manager in a showroom tells her, for example, about the usefulness of wheel locks to prevent stealing, she may buy them too. Here, a customer finds out about her need during the communication process. A similar situation is possible in the corporate sector. So, if a company has several people working on outgoing calls, obviously, it makes sense to implement a cost-effective IP-telephony. This will reduce expenses and allow the productivity of managers to be tracked. The company's management may not be aware of the IP-telephony benefits. But if a salesperson of IP-systems manages to bring management a message about the way they can save money by using IP-telephony and carries out the further sales process correctly – that can be a deal!

The **interest** of a buyer is another important criterion for determining purchase potential. For consumer sales, this factor may play a crucial role, especially when the sum of a purchase is not too large. However, when it comes to corporate sales, hardly is the interest ever the main and sufficient factor. When I started my career, it had seemed to me that having an interest is a great reason to buy. Alas! These dreams lie in ruins of reality. Some customers are very interested and some of them are just great enthusiasts when it comes to something new. But this does not mean that a purchase will be made immediately or even made at all.

A budget for purchase is the best criterion for products with flexible pricing. If a salesperson understands how much money a person is willing to spend, that's a great step toward making a decision. For example, buyers of travelling services do not hide their budget. This helps a seller to suggest the best offer for them. However, for the corporate sector, the budget cannot always be disclosed. Sometimes, this is due to the fact that if a budget is mentioned, the position of a customer in the bargaining process becomes weaker. Sometimes, financial planning may be flexible: it may answer a proposal but does not dictate it. Not intending to be rude about the budget and not to jump the gun, a lead generation manager may ask whether any budget at all is allocated for this type of product. This will enable the evaluation of purchase possibility and the seriousness of a lead's approach. Moreover, experienced sales managers can approximately predict the budget of their potential customers, based on turnover and business type.

Purchase timeframe is another important criterion for lead qualification. It is particularly important for pricey products. If customers are planning an expensive purchase, they are likely to understand when they can buy it. (Exceptions include luxury goods that are sometimes bought spontaneously.) If purchase timeframe is not defined, it's likely that we have a low potential customer at the moment. The average purchase life-cycle differs for different products. For example, it usually takes 15-40 minutes to decide about a car rental service. Selecting a program of medical insurance may take one or two weeks. That's enough time to study the main proposals in the market and choose the most worthy, to speak to insurance companies, and plan a day for completing a contract. For different corporate products, a purchase decision timeframe may vary from several minutes to several years. Mainly, it depends on the decision-making process in a company and the number of confirming authorities.

Here, we come to the last criterion: a person's **authority role within the decision-making process.** This option is especially important for corporate lead generation and sales. There are usually several persons involved in a decision-making process. For example, one of them can initiate a purchase and be responsible for the final choice. The second one makes a request for proposals, searches for providers, and negotiates with them. The third one confirms the budget. The fourth one gives the final approval. Yes, every authority may decline your proposal. The fewer the number of persons involved, the easier the process of making a decision to purchase is. (However, this fact does not guarantee that you get great sales conversion and ROI among companies with a single decision maker). At the same time, there are consumer sales where a decision is also influenced by several persons. Examples are large family purchases like immovable properties, cars, and education. Every member of a family has his or her own reasons and motivation. As a result, they need different arguments. Taking this into account may allow you to attain more leads and close more sales.

To qualify a lead, you need to prepare a **list of qualifying questions.** These questions should help to identify necessary information before transferring a lead to the next stage of sales. Responses are usually scored from 0 to 5. This scoring system may at first seem too complicated. However, it is necessary when several people are involved in interactions with a customer during a sales cycle. This scoring system will help to identify the hottest leads for active sales and those who should be for now just nurtured. Obtaining such information will enhance the effectiveness of further lead interaction. It helps to understand at what stage of the purchasing cycle a possible customer is and to allocate him or her appropriate sales or nurturing activities. As a result, you will be able to address them in the best way possible and hit the target with less effort.

Getting **answers to qualifying questions** via phone enables you to attain the most detailed information, as a lead generation manager can personally clarify all the possibilities. There is also the possibility to ask people visiting your landing page to fill in a questionnaire (with a bonus to everyone who does). Another option is a proactive search for customers with special needs by using special innovative web services like market places and social network monitoring tools. Choosing a method is a matter of price and the communication channel your target prospective customers choose. If a target audience is narrow and you do not want to miss anyone, you should call. If you are interested only in hot leads and are assured you will get enough leads without live communication, use other less pricey methods.

I see that you have some concerns already, haven't you? A **lead may not want to share information**. Yes, this may happen. A lead generation manager should not insist that a lead reveal information. These questions should be asked very carefully so as to not scare off potential buyers. So choose the politest words or ask indirect questions. After all, the lead has not confirmed a willingness to buy yet and has only expressed a preliminary interest in some category of goods. For example, do not ask "How much money do you want to spend?" but, rather ask: "What budget do you think will suit you for this type of product?" These questions should leave a customer the option to either answer you about the facts or not – a person has every right to remain silent. Yes, everything one says will be used to speed up the purchase.

You can achieve a **buyer's frankness** if you honestly say that you need this information to make the best offer. Having understood someone's position and background, you can make a proposal that best fits that person's needs, interests, and budget. You are playing on their side. And even if a person **refuses to give answers to some questions**, this is still **valuable** for future sales. No information is also informative. Perhaps people do not know what they want. This reduces the likelihood of a sale, but this tells you that these clients may need some nurturing (depending on all other qualifying questions). It may also be that some people just need personal contact before revealing this information, and this lead should still be taken through the sales process. There is a vague difference between these answers; a lead generation manager should be a good psychologist to understand this difference. There are also innovative products for which **customers do not know they have a need or an interest** until they have information from a company, which leaves them in a state of revelation. Having no answers to any lead generation questions is still more informative than not asking any questions at all.

Let's illustrate the aforementioned information with an example: **a lead qualification scoring system for a company that provides information security software and consulting**. In this case, lead generation was done by arranging business meetings with leads. We used various methods: cold calling, personal e-mails, and LinkedIn. Lead generation managers had to clarify a need, an interest, a budget situation, and an authority role. The following table shows some variations of questions asked and an interpretation of results:

№	Lead Qualification Criteria	Lead Qualification for a Security Software Provider	
		Variations of Questions asked via Phone	**Result Scoring**
1	Need	"As far as I understand, your current security system does not suit your goals. Have you already determined other challenges that need addressed? (…) Have you determined the system requirements?" "If I understand you correctly, you do not use any network security software currently? Have you already formulated the functional requirements? Do you have some RFP[9] or can I send you a questionnaire?"	5 points – strong need and product requirements are defined; 4 points – moderate need and most requirements are defined; 3 points – weak need and some requirements are defined; 2 points – weak need and no requirements are defined; 1 point – no need.
2	Interest	"Previously, have you already considered such solutions? (…) What products and features were of interest?" "Have you addressed a similar challenge before? What is your priority for the functionality of such solutions? (I am asking so we can focus on this during the meeting.)"	5 points – strong interest; 4 points – moderate interest; 3 points – neutral position; 2 points – skeptical; 1 point – prefers another supplier.
3	Decision timeframe	"What do you think is, potentially, in case our meeting goes well and you think the functionality of the product suits you, the timeframe in your company for making such purchases?"	5 points – 3 months (a client can make a decision in the next 3 months and wants to meet with the provider as soon as possible); 4 points – 6 months and ready to meet in the next

---

[9] RFP – request for proposal

		"If there is interest after the meeting, tell me, please, how does the purchase authorization process in your company usually go? How long does the process usually take?"	month; 3 points – 12 months and ready to meet the next 3 months; 2 points – more than 12 months; 1 point – no defined timeframe exists.
4	Budget	"Can I ask you if there is any defined budget for the project?" "If there might be a demand for this service, have you previously allocated a specific budget for it?" "Haven't you considered such a project before and fixed budget frames? I am asking this in order to prepare the best proposal in terms of functionality."	5 points – budget is approved; 4 points – budget is expected to be approved; 3 points – budget is negotiated; 2 points – need to ask for a budget and a possibility of its allocation is quite fair; 1 point – no budget at least for the next 12 months.
5	Authority role	"Tell me, please, in case of success, how is further confirmation usually conducted? Do I understand correctly that you prepare a proposal for your colleagues? Who else is involved in this decision-making process?" "Tell me, please, will anyone else attend the meeting or participate in future cooperation with our team? Who else will be involved in the decision-making process?"	5 points – the main/final approval; 4 points – preparation of requirements; 3 points – recommendation role; 2 points – minor role, advising; 1 point – no role.

Then, we **calculate the scores for each lead.** This allows us to quickly determine lead quality and categorize it as:
- 20-25 points – a hot lead;
- 13-19 points – a warm lead;
- 7-12 points – a cold lead;
- 5-6 – a prospect or a disqualified lead.

Hot leads should move into the sales process for personal business meetings and direct negotiations. These are the meetings of primary importance. After these meetings, sales managers prepare commercial proposals in the shortest terms. **Warm leads** are also treated individually. However, they are a second priority (although there may be exceptions – in case of highly profitable opportunities or strategically important deals). During personal meetings, a salesperson has a chance to demonstrate to the customers all the benefits of the proposal. In addition, there is a chance to upsell and increase the original scope of a project. Cold leads proceed to the nurturing stage to gain a higher probability rate; however, in the case of interesting prospects or free resources of sales managers, some of these leads can move to live meetings. It depends on the type of goods sold and their price. Disqualified customers can be added to some neutral nurturing activity like newsletter subscription. This is the most economical way to stay in touch with your target audience.

© Lead Generation: Theory and Practice by Ksenia Andreeva

Here is another example of how **consumer goods leads can be qualified**. For example, let's have a look at the organic food sector. Organic products are quite an expensive category of food. One farmer sold them directly to customers. He wanted to find a narrow audience of people living in a city near his farm who were ready to pay more for healthy food. His goal was to create awareness in this narrow sector and gain the personal loyalty of well-heeled people thinking about their health. Also, his customers were returning ones. Therefore, there was an emphasis on investing some resources to find these potential customers. For lead generation, the farmer used a marketing survey form that was placed on the farm's website and on landings created for a Google campaign, and organized promotional give-outs in one of the city's malls. People were encouraged to fill in the form by participation in a lottery – a winner would receive a food basket with dairy products and seasonal fruits. Below are the questions of the survey:

№	Lead Qualification Criteria	Lead Qualification for an Organic Farm	
		Questions (in a questionnaire on the website or offline)	Answer Scoring
1	Need	How often do you buy organic food? A – regularly, once or twice a week; B – one or two times a month; C – rarely, but I would like to buy it more often; D – no, and I do not plan to.	4 points – A; 3 points – B; 2 points – C; 1 point – D.
2	Interest	What organic and farm food do you buy or plan to buy? A – milk products; B – meat; B – fruits and vegetables; G – grocery; D – none of them.	3 points – 2 or more variants; 1 point – one variant; 0 points – D.
3	Budget	What budget do you spend on a monthly basis for organic food? A – less than $50; B – $50-100; C – $100-300; D – $300 or more.	4 points – D; 3 points – C; 2 points – B; 1 point – A.

Lead qualification for this farmer is calculated by the following scoring:
- 8-11 points – a hot lead;
- 4-5 – a warm lead;
- 2-3 points – a cold lead;
- 0 points – a prospect or a disqualified lead.

All collected cold leads went to the nurturing stage where there were cost-effective activities (such as e-mail marketing and direct mail) that informed people about the benefits of organic products and a healthy lifestyle. As for warm and hot leads, it was sensible to invest more in attracting them; for example, they were invited to the farm, sent printed booklets with recipes of dishes that could be prepared, and invited to participate in a taste test.

While a lead may achieve a **high score** by qualification criteria, this **does not guarantee that a sale will happen.** Lead generation will allow you to find prospective customers, to evaluate their willingness to buy, and to create a pool of hot and warm leads. The rest depends on your sales force and product features.

The marketing, lead generation, and sales departments must agree on qualification criteria before the start of any activity. It should not scare you that sometimes after the launching of an activity, it becomes evident that it is necessary to adjust the criteria: to add or to clarify one of answers, for example. This is absolutely fine; conducting lead generation means always working in a test mode.

Lead Nurturing: What Goes Around Comes Around

Cold leads with which you have no chance to close a deal or prospects whose decision is delayed for too long are transferred to a stage of **lead nurturing.** It is important not to lose these contacts. After all, a large amount of work was done to find them or to attract them. In a corporate sector, there is a rule: 45% of all the leads sooner or later become clients. The trick is with this meaningful "sooner or later." After all, a process of transformation from a cold lead into a client may take several years. But for companies operating in narrow markets, it is especially important to ensure the loyalty of every potential customer.

There is no sense pushing cold leads in the same manner as hot and warm ones, for two reasons. First, it will **distract sales managers from closing leads with high potential deals.** Second, **cold leads are still at a stage when they are not ready to purchase,** and trying to convince them otherwise is useless, unless your goods might be purchased spontaneously. But if you push too hard, you may lose an opportunity. Recall the classical AIDA[10] sales model where A = attention, I = interest, D = desire, and A = action. Cold leads are somewhere between attention and interest. So your interaction with these prospective customers should

---

[10]According to BusinessDictionary.Com, AIDA (acronym for Attention, Interest, Desire and Action) is the names for steps to be taken sequentially in a selling process. The salesperson must (1) first make the prospect aware of the product, (2) foster any interest shown, (3) stimulate the desire to buy and possess the product and, finally, (4) encourage action to purchase.
http://www.businessdictionary.com/definition/AIDA-selling-system.html#ixzz3tHmwIQAe

include reminding them about your services and products, and providing them with valuable information to trigger desire and provoke action.

The purpose of lead nurturing is to be in touch with a potential lead and to be nearby when a person is ready to buy. When, finally, a definite need arises, the name of your company should emerge in the person's head. The nurturing strategy depends on your type of business. Companies develop their own methods, including several successive "touch points" with a potential customer. These touch points are designed to increase their awareness and loyalty to your company. The following are **possible lead nurturing activities**:
- e-mail newsletters;
- valuable content like white papers, tutorials and e-books;
- stories about other people or companies using your goods;
- webinars and podcasts;
- offline events;
- contests, raffles, quizzes;
- social media marketing;
- invitations to marketing surveys and result sharing;
- industry trends;
- holiday greetings;
- personal letters and phone calls from time to time;
- give-aways and souvenirs;
- offline mailings;
- free samples and demos;
- personal letters by top managers.

Nurturing is a **full-value lead generation channel**, which should be used to attain maximum results. It allows you to address people with an identified need (however a low one) and gradually prepare their interest. At the same time, a very small number of companies use nurturing tactics. Perhaps the reason for this is that marketers and sales managers need to show immediate success. They do not have the strength and patience for the long-term goals. It is like "After me, the deluge."[11] Yes, the temptation to have a "bird in the hand" is great. Nonetheless, consistent interaction with low potential customers will provide a good return over time. Furthermore, there are various automated tools that make this work easier and faster; we will speak about them later.

---

[11] "Après moi, le déluge" ("After me, the deluge") means "I care not what happens when I am dead and gone." This is a famous quote of Madame de Pompadour, the mistress of Louis XV (1722–1764).

Sales and Lead Generation: Shaken, Not Stirred

Sales and lead generation should be considered separate tasks. These are **different activities, each with its own objectives, methods, and results.** It is one thing to find and attract new customers, and another to close sales. Separation of sales and lead generation should be done first when setting different goals for each task. In addition, it is very effective to have different business owners for both processes, if the size and structure of your business allows it.

The difference between sales and lead generation is the following. For lead generation, the most important thing is to understand who among your suspects has a chance to purchase. Having found or attracted a lead, you need to fix the result and move on to the next. And to do this quickly! Thus, this work **requires even more communication skills than sales. However, it is more widespread.** This does not downgrade the importance of this job. Lead generation managers, surely, must have a good grasp of the products they promote. But this knowledge should not distract them from searching or attracting as many prospective customers as possible and establishing contact with them.

In direct sales, everything is all the other way around. This requires a deeper **investment in each client** than in lead generation. Sales work necessitates an excellent understanding of customer motives and goals. A sales manager must be able to convince and negotiate. If there are chances for a large deal, most of time a sales manager may be occupied with a single customer. And this makes sense. Good salespeople are as valuable as gold; they are either hard to find or it takes a lot of time and effort to grow them. Therefore, these professionals should be used for their intended purpose. They need to make money – close the deal. As Alec Baldwin in the Glengarry Glen Ross movie said: "ABC. A – always, B – be, C – closing. Always be closing!"

Lead generation is a **marketing activity.** It is logical to have lead generation people as part of a marketing department. Sales managers may be involved in drafting a plan for lead generation, defining lead criteria, setting quantitative and qualitative goals, etc. Then the lead generation and/or the marketing department organizes various activities that need to result in getting the contact information of new potential buyers. Then, the sales department takes hot and warm leads into an active phase and holds talks, while other leads go to the nurturing phase. If a hot or a warm lead delays a decision for a long time, it makes sense to return it to marketing for nurturing. In some businesses, there is a third level of sales as well – when a contract is signed, a client goes to a customer service or project department, which has a brilliant opportunity to sell him or her something else. This scheme is provided below:

Pic. 9. Three-level structure of lead generation and sales process

Thus, a company may have a **two-level or three-level structure**. In such an organization, each group focuses on its responsibility. This results in having a sales system where **your managers can easily make sales and leverage company profit**. Being focused on warm and hot leads, sales managers work more efficiently in terms of sales volume. At the same time, the company benefits because of its smooth business processes.

It is important that the **dependency on the human factor is reduced**. This means that in case of sudden sick leave or discharging of any manager, the whole mechanism will not break down. After all, if one manager is looking for new leads and at the same time closes deals, his or her absence could be very painful for business. By dividing lead generation and sales functions, a company is protected from data loss in the event of someone's dismissal or resignation. So keep your sales and lead generation apart, *divide et impera*![12]

In addition, the allocation of responsibilities between lead generation and sales creates optimal working conditions. A company helps its employees to better perform their duties – to find more customers and close more deals. Managers become more likely to get bonuses for great results. In addition to promoting collaboration with marketing, sales managers achieve favorable conditions when a marketing department finds new qualified leads. Hence, an employee's loyalty to his or her company increases.

---

[12] Divide et impera (Latin, divide and rule) are the words of Traiano Boccalini, Italian satirist (1556 – 1613), in La bilancia politica, which serves as a common principle in politics. The use of this technique is meant to empower the sovereign to control subjects, populations, or factions of different interests, who collectively might be able to oppose his rule. Source: Wikipedia (https://en.wikipedia.org/wiki/Divide_and_rule)

Micro small businesses may not have any human resources for separation of sales, lead generation, and marketing functions. However, even for these companies, it makes sense to understand the difference between sales and lead generation and to treat both tasks separately. Simply speaking, do not mix lead generation and sales results. Otherwise, your company's future may be like this joke: one sales manager meets another. One asks:
- How are things going?
- Great! I have done 100 calls, have sent 200 letters, and have made 10 commercial proposals.
- That's clear. I haven't closed any sales either.

Budgeting Lead Generation and Lead Cost

Lead generation effectiveness is measured not only by the quality and quantity of leads, but also their **cost**. The financial aspect is very important. You should allocate a reasonable amount for lead generation that balances the cost of leads with the profit acquired at the end of the sales campaign.

Let's see what influences the cost of a lead. The **obvious expenses for subcontractors** are a cost factor for leads. Examples may include contact list acquisition and participation in an exhibition or call center service. These expenses are transparent enough.

The second category of expenses is **the materials required for a lead generation activity**. For example, these are brochures and handouts at events, prizes for filling in application forms and copywriting services. Of course, there will be long-term materials, which you purchase once and utilize often. For example, a white paper that may be downloaded on your landing page for a pay per click campaign on Google may also be used in a direct-mailing activity for your partners' event registration list. These long-term materials are investments that can be utilized in several main activities. While some may overlook these materials, taking them for granted, the important thing is not to miss these investments at all.

The next factor is **employee labor**. Employees' time is very important! **Your financial department or accounting department** can suggest how to calculate the cost of your employees' hourly wage. You can ask these departments for assistance in obtaining average figures – perhaps they will find time to do so, if you explain the importance of the issue. Otherwise, you will have to calculate it yourself, taking into account the following:

- salaries and employee bonuses;
- various taxes;
- sick leave;
- insurance;
- office and working place;
- software and hardware;
- office expenses;
- training.

In any case, you need an **average cost per man-hour**. This average can be used as a constant for further evaluations without needing further recalculation. Having a common approach in estimating labor costs is important so that you do not waste time on fixing minor variations in the estimation process.

The amount of time that managers spend on lead generation activities **influences the return on a marketing investment**. For example, e-mailing usually takes a small amount of time, while participation in an exhibition is much more time-consuming; preparing a booth and marketing pieces, thinking creatively, working through a registration list (if it is available), and announcing your participation for prospective customers demands more time and hours of investment, not to mention the event itself. Therefore, due to such time investment, these activities should provide the maximum number of new leads.

Let me provide **another example**. To gather suspects' contact information just by surfing the web takes long hours. Because of the amount of time required and the hourly wage invested, it may be more cost-effective to buy a database from a business list provider. Making a large volume of offline mailings using your company's own materials is also time-consuming and costly. Thus, it is often cheaper to outsource this task to a direct marketing agency.

To calculate labor costs for a particular lead generation activity, you can use the following method:

Calculation of Labor Hours for Lead Generation Activities			
Activity	Outsource of Telemarketing	Ads in Google	One-Day Exhibition
The number of labor-hours in detail	- preparation of materials for a call script = 2-3 labor-hours; - call script check = 3-4 labor-hours; - remotely controlling telemarketers and	- preparation of an advertising campaign = 5-7 labor-hours; - payment and organization issues = 1 labor-hour; - landing page	- preparing a booth (design, equipment) = 5-6 labor-hours; - printing brochures to give out = 1-2 labor-hours); - souvenirs = 1-3 labor-hours; - team coordination =

	checking results = 8-10 labor-hours; - preparation of the final contact list to be imported into CRM = 3-12 labor-hours; - interaction with a call center (negotiations, contract, payment) = 3 labor-hours.	creation = 8 labor-hours; - tracking analytics, testing, and corrections = 30 min/day during a month.	1-2 labor-hours; - booth set-up = 4 labor-hours; - working the event = 8 labor-hours for 3 employees; - de-installation = 2 labor-hours; - communications with organizers (booth selection, contract, payment, etc.) = 3 labor-hours; - follow-up calls and e-mails = 4 labor-hours.
Total labor-hours	~2.5 + 3.5 + 9 + 7 + 3 = 25 labor-hours	~15 + 20 x 0.5 = 20 labor-hours	~5.5 + 1.5 + 2 + 1.5 + 4 + 8 x 3 + 2 + 3 + 4 = 47.5 labor-hours
Cost of 1 labor-hour	$17/1 labor-hour		
Expenses for labor-hours spent	25 x 17 = $425	20 x 17 = $340	47.5 x 17 = $807.5
Additional expenses for subcontractors	$2,200 (call center services)	$1,400 (clicks and a subcontractor for landing page creation)	$10,000 (booth and registration fees)
Expenses for marketing materials	$0	$500 (landing page)	$2,000 (turn-key booth, extra equipment, design, give-outs)
Total expenses per lead generation activity	= 425 + 2 200 + 0 = $2,625	= 340 + 1400 + 500 = $2,240	= 807.5 + 10 000 + 2 000 = $12,807.5

By understanding the final cost of doing any activity and calculating the number of leads, you can determine the price of a lead. This is what is the most important for you as far as lead generation is concerned. It is important to understand this determination when you compare the **cost per lead** in different marketing activities and when you evaluate the prices of lead generation agencies. When you deal with lead generation and marketing services, aside from cost per lead, you may encounter the following pricing principles:
- cost per click;
- cost per impressions (CPI) or, to be correct, per thousand of

impressions;
- cost per contact of your target group;
- cost per e-mail sent;
- cost per e-mail answered by a recipient;
- cost per action (CPA), for example, an answer to a questionnaire;
- cost per delegate;
- cost per business meeting.

Some of these figures mostly coincide with the cost per lead, for example, the last two items of the above list. Other figures should be treated as intermediary results on the way to leads.

PART 2. PRACTICE OF LEAD GENERATION

Lead Generation Methods
Overview

Do you remember the striking scene with a swordsman during Indiana Jones' "Raiders of the Lost Ark"? Here, Indiana Jones, having survived an elaborate chase through a casbah, is confronted by an Arab swordsman whipping through a flashy routine with a scimitar. Indy initially squares off against the deadly swordsman, bearing only his trademark whip in his hands; then, with a look of infinite fatigue and disgust, he casually pulls out his revolver and blows the bad guy away. Ba-hah! Using this example, we see that Indiana has chosen the right weapon. Channeling our inner Indiana, we acknowledge that it's important to choose the **right marketing tools**.

Below, I divide the main types of lead generation activities into **four groups**:
1. **Live communication and by phone:**
    - telesales/telemarketing;
    - appointments of business meetings;
    - industry shows and conferences;
    - events hosted by your company;
    - marketing surveys.
2. **Mailings:**
    - e-mail marketing;
    - offline direct mail, letters, and flyers;
    - subscribers of mass media and related websites;

- SMS mailing.
3. **Internet:**
    - corporate website for getting leads;
    - search engines;
    - social networks;
    - relevant online resources.
4. **Offline advertising** with elements of lead generation:
    - advertising in media (print, radio, TV);
    - outdoor and indoor advertising in public places.

In the aforementioned list, I do not include anything related to purely brand advertising and PR, which fails to acknowledge how dual-purpose activities can be used to gain leads. **Brand awareness generally requires different tools** and it has a different purpose that is not the focus of our attention.

Now, let's have a look at the methods indicated as the most successful by the respondents of the Lead Generation Benchmark Report.

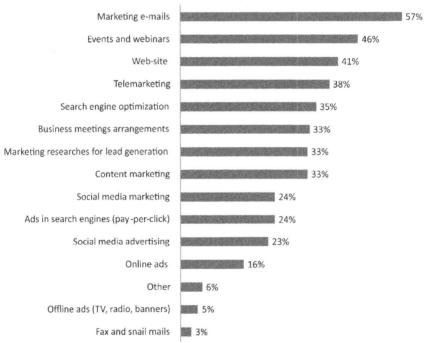

Pic. 10. Which activities were the most effective for lead generation in 2015?
Source: © NWComm. A Benchmark Report on Lead Generation Strategies and Tactics for 2015-2016

Fifty-seven percent of respondents state that marketing e-mails, events, and webinars are the most effectual methods; telemarketing is another popular option, mentioned by 38% of those surveyed. In the realm of offline advertisements, faxes, and postal ("snail") mail yielded only a small portion of success, 5% and 3% respectively.

As for future plans for 2016, the respondents had provided the following information:

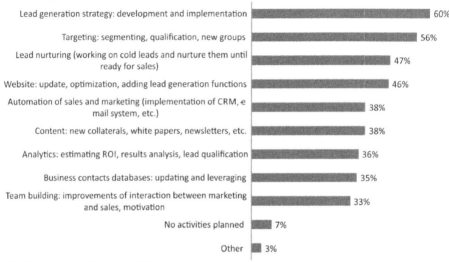

Pic. 11. What does your company plan to do for lead generation in 2016?
Source: © NWComm. A Benchmark Report on Lead Generation Strategies and Tactics for 2015-2016

Pic. 12. Which type of marketing campaigns do you plan to do for lead generation in 2016?
Source: © NWComm. A Benchmark Report on Lead Generation Strategies and Tactics for 2015-2016

Below I shall describe each lead generation tool in detail. It is important for you to put all the leads found into **CRM** (Customer Relationship Management) or you may use a different method to keep them organized, making it possible to indicate which marketing activity has brought them. This will help to track a lead up to purchase and enable an analysis of the used methods' effectiveness.

The sequence and general pace of lead generation actions is called the cadence. It is essentially the **regular rhythm of executing of calls, newsletters, personalized e-mails, and invitations to events**. Your cadence should reflect the type of the product you sell, and there can be varying cadences for different target groups. A cadence is used actively in e-mail, but its principles are also applied to multi-channel marketing including phone calls, social media, events, and offline letters.

For example, a **cadence for a business meeting appointment** for the B2B sector may be as follows:
- Day 1: An introduction letter with a proposal of a business meeting.
- Day 2: A call to ask about the meeting, and an e-mail with detailed information.
- Day 6: A call to obtain an agreement and to identify an interest.
- Day 8 A reminder letter to agree on a meeting and to identify an interest.
- Day 12: A call to get an agreement and to identify an interest.

The sequence of actions in a cadence is influenced by **triggers**. For example, when someone opens an e-mail, it is a good reason to send him or her one more. At the same time, when people pay no attention to e-mails for a long time, it is possible that there is no point in sending more as it may only annoy your potential respondent.

First of all, following a cadence helps lead generation managers **average their attempts to reach any one party**. Managers will address all contacts with an approximately equal number of efforts. This means that each prospect will receive an appropriate number of calls and e-mails; not more, and not less. This way, you can avoid a situation where some prospects receive dozens of calls, while others receive just one call and a single e-mail.

Second, the introduction of cadence enables the **optimization of all the actions required to obtain the maximum number of leads**. For example, having fulfilled the number of actions addressed to a suspect, you will find up to 90% results are driven by a cadence including six calls and two e-mails. This means that a lead generation manager should presumably stop at the seventh call and leave these prospects alone (at least, for some time).

Creating the best cadence for your sales campaign requires time and effort. It is essential to understand that cadence is **not about the frequency of contact or its type** (e.g. "the more calls the better"). It is about finding the best scheme of "touching" your customers, giving them enough time to think about your proposal, and at the same time not so much time that they may be prone to forget about your offer.

Constant testing is also a necessity. Take small samples and work with them. Experiment with different texts, calculate the number of bounces and responses, take into account the feedback from potential customers, improve your advertising message, and try new communications channels.

Good Old Telesales

Cold calls are one of the most popular types of telemarketing. They provide a wide coverage of the target audience and enable contact with narrow groups of people. Here you get immediate feedback from your suspects, and the person calling can clarify information if necessary. Now we shall talk about telesales – these are cold calls that have the primary goal of making a sale on the phone without any intermediate steps such as arranging business meetings or presenting an invitation to an event.

I must admit that there has been an **"overheating" in the sphere of sales over the phone**. It is becoming more and more difficult to call new people and talk to them. Buyers of consumer products often perceive calls as an intrusion into their personal space. In the US, for example, the Federal Trade Commission has created a National Do Not Call List. It includes a number of people who demand telemarketers never call them. Each call center is required to check with this list prior to conducting calls.

Even your **own customers**, if you are not constantly in contact with them by phone, do not always welcome an incoming call. This is confirmed, for example, by the experience of banks that try to sell new services to their customers. Making calls on behalf of an unknown contractor is even more difficult because of the possible negative reaction on the other end. Some secretaries refuse to transfer a call to the company's employer if a caller does not know his or her name or makes a call for the first time.

Does it make sense to **break the telesales process into two distinct operations** – lead generation and actual sales? It depends on the specifics of products sold. If they are not as plain as day and require a long interaction with a potential customer – yes, definitely. If the number of cold calls per month is more than a thousand – yes, it is better to divide communication via phone into two stages. Otherwise, the sales process will distract a telemarketer from dialing other prospective customers. As a result, approaching the target audience will slow down, if not completely die. But if sales are needed in a small volume, separation does not make sense. If you have a transparent price list, separation will only complicate the process. Plus, your potential customers may be displeased by the fact that they are transferred to a new person with whom it is necessary to re-establish contact.

The first step of beginning telesales is to make a **contact list.** (I shall come back later to the ways we can accomplish this.) The list should not include contacts that you already have established, contacts that have refused, or contacts that are your current customers (unless you want to sell these customers additional services). If you have a CRM, you can track such statuses to exclude these contacts. If you work with a narrow target group, this list must be approved by the people engaged in direct sales. Perhaps, they will cut more contacts for their own reasons; for example, these people may know if a suspect works with a competitor or is going to be a bankrupt.

The next important step is to prepare a **call script and letter samples.** These materials should reflect the primary features of your service and appeal to the most important motives of decision makers regarding purchase. A call script also should deal with the main objections. An e-mail is usually sent after a phone call to clarify and support your proposal. This is especially important for complex products that need to be studied for some time. I shall speak more on these issues in a chapter concerning marketing pieces.

If your target group is narrow and **you have a valuable customer,** do not hesitate to invest time in this customer and use other methods of contact, such as telephone or e-mail, to reach him or her. If a suspect does not respond by phone or by e-mail, you can write a message on a **professional social network,** like LinkedIn. I would not recommend Facebook for business purposes, as it serves personal goals and some people may consider it unethical to be disturbed on their private platform. Do not spoil the first impression. Sometimes (rarely, but occasionally, it happens), decision makers even of a C-level can be reached via a feedback form on a website. It also happens that an e-mail sent to a general company's address may provide a result. Do not neglect anything. Success is never blamed! The only contact method that is used less often today is fax. Sending such a message is equivalent to sending a letter to the trash.

~~~ *Tip* ~~~

Sometimes, the names of the persons required can be found in press releases or in news (Google helps). If you still do not know the name of the person you are calling and cannot find it and the secretary does not let you through without a name, try to call in two stages. Call the first time and introduce yourself as the employee of a referral service who is checking the name for a professional directory. The next day, call for your purpose. Another method (a cheat actually, but better than nothing) to get the name is to act through a PR department and ask for someone's opinion on an article.

~~~

When conducting calls on your own (not with the help of an outsourcing call center), you need to pay attention to the following aspects:

- The **number of calls made per day**. This can be monitored through special call center software.
- Daily or weekly **qualitative results** on leads, refuses, new contacts, information sent, delayed decisions. No matter what software you use for it, each contact should have a status update. It is even possible to change statuses in Excel, but checking this every day and preparing analytics manually will be too time-consuming.
- The level of **professionalism a telesales person** exhibits for cold call techniques and in conversation. Here, you just listen to the manager and give feedback.
- The quality of recordings in CRM or any other form accepted in

your company. This is particularly important for newbie employees.

- The quality of a contact list: how many contacts are out of date and need updating? If you have bought a contact list from a business information supplier you can apply for a replacement of irrelevant information with a new list.

- The **reaction of potential clients:** what questions do they ask? What doubts do they express? This is important information when correcting a call script, and, perhaps, even for refining the position of your products.

- **Final quantitative results regarding new leads and sales volume.**

For lead generation completed via cold calls, it is much more effective to achieve a level of professionalism which makes the person you are calling think you are not a telemarketer. **Nobody enjoys speaking to a cyborg that makes 500 calls per day**. A call should sound like a call made by a live **highly professional person who occupies some concrete position, a representative of a company with a specific corporate style**. I would dare to say – with a personality! This call should be done with the person who we call in mind; the person should not be a characterless line or #342 of a contact list. The manager calling should sound as if he or she has a general understanding of the business situation. Boilerplate speech and reading text are easily recognized and they often cause a negative reaction from the person with whom you are speaking. Of course, the style of a conversation must remain businesslike and the speech should be well-bred; communication manners should remain polite. However, emotions, humor, sympathy and other expressions of individuality may only improve the result of a call. The most important thing in establishing first contact is to do it positively – here a personal approach always works wonders! Although, of course, we need to pick up on what mood the person has on the other end and should not overenthusiastically perform.

The necessity of telemarketers being able to speak by phone and not read makes it hard to find a call center that can provide such professionals. At first, a **call center seems to be the best option**. Unfortunately, for telesales at the executive level, most of them are only good as far as the amount of calls is concerned. The style of conversation is a problem for most telemarketers. For example, our agency has acquired former call center employees, and the first thing we did was train them to speak over the phone properly. While at call centers, these employees conducted 500 calls per day; however, they were unable to have a phone conversation. We had to make them stop the needless chattering that arose from following call scripts. We trained them to make live conversation over the phone. According to one such employee, our method was "a new way to call," and, for the first time, he was kind of perplexed. The man could not get used to the fact that a phone call can be a natural conversation and not reading the script from the beginning to end. A natural speech manner brings the maximum number of potential customers.

Telesales Main Actions

- Identify the target audience and lead qualification criteria.
- Prepare the contact list.
- Prepare the call script and e-mail.
- Choose a form of reporting (e.g., CRM).
- Test calls on a small sample.
- Adjust the call script and e-mail.
- Active calling.
- Find leads and qualify them.
- Active sales.
- Transfer of cold leads to nurturing phase.
- Analyze results, calculate the conversion rate and ROI.

Let's have a closer look at one activity realized with the help of a lead generation agency. Here we can see that lead generation can serve the goals of **environmental charity organizations** as well. This particular enterprise is concerned with climate change, deforestation, overfishing, commercial whaling, which are humanitarian concerns. These issues certainly need adequate funding. The policy of this organization is not to accept any funding from any government or commercial corporation. In order to find funding, the organization constantly attracts private donations that are usually provided by interested individuals. This campaign's purpose was to attract people wishing to make a donation and identify major donors in a particular city.

In the **preparation stage**, training materials and a written script of the campaign's motivation have been developed for telemarketers. In addition to raising funds, a call script should popularize an organization's mission, values, and objectives for its target audience. Test calls were then made to determine which variation of the call script was the best. Outgoing calls and follow-up e-mails were completed. The team used predictive dialing to reduce time on calls. Ongoing training and constant feedback from the project manager to the team resulted in a significant quality improvement.

At the project's conclusion, the following **results** were obtained. During six months of the project, a target audience of 60,000 was contacted by phone and 27% of them agreed to donate. 4% of the 60,000 actually made donations, averaging $11. The conversion from leads to sales was 15%: 2,400 people became donors. Everyone who made a donation then has received a thank you call on behalf of the organization.

During the first stage of the project, the return on investment was negative. This loss was due to the high cost of attracting donators via phone and the small amount received in donations. The negative ROI can also be explained by a problem encountered in the first stage of the project. Donations were initially not accepted by SMS, which stopped people who did not want to send a donation with their credit card. This issue was fixed by the second stage, and conversion improved significantly. At the end of the project, the **ROI was positive and averaged 25.**

Parameter	Telesales for the environmental organization
Suspects	60,000 people
Positive response (agreed to donate)	27%
Leads	16,200 people
Donators ("sales")	2,400 people
Percentage of donators to suspects	=2,400/60,000 *100%= 4%
Conversion from leads to donators	= 2,400/16,200 *100% = 15%
Average donation ("sale")	$11
ROI	25

Matchmaking: The Key to a Customer

For products and services that have sales which require personal negotiations with customers, **arranging a business meeting** (or a conference call) **is the best way to secure a client**. Many managers who conduct active personal sales believe that the only purpose of a phone call is to agree to a meeting. I support this opinion for the sales of expensive products with flexible specifications. These sales may be corporate services (consulting, wholesale, production) or expensive products sold to consumers (individual tourism, events services, etc.). Decisions about their purchase require some time and thought. Therefore, the best way to speed up the process and persuade customers to purchase is to speak to them in person.

Typically, sales managers **arrange new meetings on their own**. I'll tell you more about this process in terms of lead generation. Sometimes, it makes sense to divide the tasks of meeting arrangements and their actual holding between the lead generation (or marketing) department and sales department. First of all, let's take apart **telesales and telemarketing, which are used to arrange business meetings**. Both methods suit different sales processes. Telesales is aimed at making sales over the phone. Matchmaking avoids telephone sales techniques, focusing only on identifying some interest from the correct target audience. Telesales are ideal for selling low-cost products with a fixed price. Matchmaking is a really effective methodology for expensive products with a discussed price and specification.

However, technically, the processes are similar. As with telesales, it is necessary to prepare and agree on a **list of contacts as well as write a call script and e-mail text**. Then, after testing is complete, the calls are started.

~~~ *Tip* ~~~
To get a cell phone number of your contact, you may use a little trick: first, give the person your cell phone number, and then, ask for his or hers. Having written your cell phone number down, your decision maker may feel that it is impolite to refuse providing his or her number (although this is not 100% guaranteed!)
~~~

The main message of lead generation telemarketers (following a brief introduction of a product and its benefits) is: "If this product is of interest to you, let's agree on a business meeting at a convenient time." Yes, it is necessary to provide basic information and to identify interest. However, do not tell everything you know, refrain from laying all the cards about competitors' drawbacks on the table, and, moreover, do not show off your erudition. If your respondent asks a lot of questions, it is likely that he or she has interest. Perfect! So, we need to persuade him or her to agree on a business meeting. Of course, there are cases when a person asks many questions and **refuses any personal meeting**. Well, the decision is entirely his or hers. Then, a telemarketer should answer all questions, and, ideally, assign a conference call with a salesperson to let the manager work directly with the contact.

After finding someone with interest, a lead generation specialist has **to qualify the lead**. Just to remind you, qualification is a process that estimates a customer's potentiality of purchase. Sometimes, leads agree to fill out a **questionnaire** before a meeting, which helps you. That's a great thing, so please always propose this option; however, do not expect anyone to fill it in or help the potential customer by phone. Depending on your industry, a questionnaire can be rather extensive – up to 10-15 questions for enterprise products.

In addition, a lead generation manager needs to coordinate some **logistics and organizational aspects of a business meeting**. Firstly, its **time** remains crucial. A lead generation manager should be aware of the sales team's current schedule for the near future and take into account the employees' wishes about preferred time and the number of meetings per day. This provides much more flexibility and speeds up appointment scheduling. It is much easier to get the desired answer to the question: "Would it be fine for you to have a meeting with my boss at 5 p.m. next Tuesday or in the first half of the day on Wednesday?" rather than "Let's have a business meeting." See the difference? The first one is a very concrete question and directs the conversation; it is similar to saying: "Please decide about only one hour of your time either on Tuesday, or on Wednesday!" The second statement is abstract and may prompt an abstract answer as well, such as "someday." **Clearly stating a question** helps my team to assign almost all the business meetings that bring our customers millions in profit. Do not hesitate. If you ask the question concretely, you will get more potential customers, and, therefore, sales.

Prior to the meeting, a lead generation specialist needs to confirm that all the parties will participate and no plans have changed. This can also be done by a sales manager. It does not really matter who does this task; the important thing is to have a common understanding of the plan of action, the agenda, and who is responsible for what. **Additional organizational details** for a meeting may include:

- **An address** where a meeting takes place. For B2C sales, your office or a neutral space like a café will be well suited. For B2B, a client's office is more appropriate and usually easy to agree on. It is better to demonstrate general awareness of the location by checking an address in advance on a website and saying something like: "You're on Charlotte Street 48, right?"

- **Attendees of the meeting**. Knowing who is attending is one of the ways to understand who is involved in the decision-making process. You can justify asking this question by saying that the knowledge is necessary for acquiring a sufficient number of brochures and handouts. Additionally, the number of participants from both sides should be balanced – if there are technical people on the other side, you should also bring yours.

- If a meeting is held in the client's office, will there be a projector and other necessary **equipment**?

- Acquire **full contact details** if you still do not have any.

A **report on a lead** with its qualification scoring is transferred to a sales manager. Having a common form agreed prior to the formation of such a report helps to avoid wasted time in refining and clarifying details.

Conference calls that are conducted via video and audio equipment are similar to a business meeting, if both parties are located in different cities. If a potential customer insists on a conference call when you offer a personal meeting, it is strange. This person is either an extreme introvert or really does not plan to purchase and wants to avoid the pressure to purchase from your side. On a more positive note, perhaps he or she may test new equipment for video conferencing☺.

Matchmaking Main Actions

- Identify the target audience and lead qualification criteria.
- Prepare the contact list.
- Prepare the call script, the e-mail, and the questionnaire.
- Choose a form of reporting (e.g., CRM).
- Test calls on a small sample.
- Adjust the call script and e-mail.
- Active calling.
- Arrange meetings and identify leads and their qualification.
- Gather feedback from sales managers after meetings.
- Active sales.
- Transfer cold leads to the nurturing phase.
- Analyze results, calculate the conversion rate, ROI.

Let's see an **example**. A company specializing in **enterprise content management systems** needed to develop a lead generation business process. Its target audience included large and medium-sized companies in the retail, production, and insurance sectors. The target title of the decision maker was at CIO or CTO level. Lead generation was completed by making business appointments, as all the sales of the company were large enough and required personal negotiations with a prospective customer.

The CEO of the company said: "In fact, there were two alternatives – to hire a new employee or to outsource an agency. We decided to try both methods at once. Very soon we saw an ineffectiveness of the first approach (at least for us) and an effectiveness of the latter. During the first week, the outsourcing agency's work led eventually to signing new contracts. In summary, after a few months, most of the meetings arranged by the agency either resulted in contracts or the contracts are still being negotiated. We have the chance to end up making sales as well."

We used cold calls and further e-mailing to arrange business meetings. A call script focused on rapidly identifying the most interested customers and asking them to arrange business meetings. Constant feedback from the company enabled the quality of leads to improve. Thus, some leads were classified as low potential, and therefore, lead criteria were adjusted. For example, the sales conversion rate could have been higher if we had only accepted leads with clarified project time terms and an allotted budget. However, this approach would have reduced a total number of leads in a long-term perspective.

The company's management wanted no more than one or two meetings per week, as each meeting required a detailed follow-up, preparing a commercial proposal, and further negotiations. So 56 business meetings and conference calls were held. Within several months, four of them led to signed contracts with a total gross profit of $53,000. The intermediate conversion rate was 7% and the return on investment – 4.7. In the future, the company will continue negotiations with the remaining clients to move them forward to the purchase cycle and increase the number of closed sales.

Parameter	Matchmaking for a Microsoft Partner
Suspects	~6000 contacts
Prospects	~110 contacts
Leads	58 meetings and conference calls
Qualified leads	56 meetings and conference calls
Number of sales	4
Conversion	4/56 = 7%
Profit	$53,000
Marketing expenses	$9,200
ROI	(53,000 – 9,200)/9,200 = 4.7

Industry Shows and Hosted Events: Better Alive

In terms of lead generation, the **effectiveness of events is determined by the people who attend** (or at least want to attend). Banners, handouts, and badges are just icing on the cake. They are important, of course. However, the main thing to have is a sufficient number of visitors from your target audience. Therefore, when deciding to participate **in an exhibition or a conference**, you should first assess its audience. Organizers of large-scale exhibitions may provide you with the demographics of visitors of last year's events and give a promotional plan or information about marketing channels used to attract various audiences. You can also see the reviews of exhibitors, media articles, photos, etc. As for **specialized professional conferences**, most organizers will show you a registration list or at least an excerpt from it (for example, a visitor's title, a company's name, and its industry). Some organizers do not disclose such information and appeal to their reputation. While I believe that a reputation is an important factor, I find true value in the lists of potential buyers within a proper target group. In fact, most attendees confirm their participation shortly before an event, so the registration list often remains very small until the last few days prior to the event. So at an early stage, organizers do not share these lists, as they do not wish to scare you. Still, it is better to try to get some information rather than none.

~~~ *Tip* ~~~
As everyone who looks into event marketing opportunities knows, sponsorship packages include something inexplicably expensive. To understand why any option costs so much, no more or less, is almost impossible. Hang around for better terms! Ask for a discount. Usually, the organizers have some flexibility in pricing and can reduce the cost for you, or provide bonus options for 10-30% of the cost to participate.
~~~

If an audience of a show seems fine, select the format of participation. The most effective thing is to agree with the organizers on **having a registration list with as many contacts as possible** a few days before the event. Ask for the list, regardless if it is final or not. If you ask for such a list, I bet that the organizers will suggest to you one of their premium sponsorship packages. It's expensive, but it's worth it. Some organizers will provide a list without contacts, but this information is valuable anyway and allows you to examine the list before the show.

By having a registration list in advance, **a lead generation manager is able to make appointments at the event** with the most interesting customers. One or two days will be spent agreeing on such brief introductory meetings; this groundwork will pay for itself. The venue of an event will become a meeting room. Be sure to ask for the cell phone number of your visitors. If a prospect walks away (which is quite possible, as every event is full of temptations like an interesting speaker or booth activity) and misses the appointment time, you will be able to phone him or her and arrange another time for your introduction.

According to my experience, a one-day event for 100 people can hold 10-20 short introductory meetings. However, it is physically demanding, so, if possible, share this pleasant burden between two sales managers. These meetings will be a rather brief introduction of approximately 10 minutes (although there are exceptions when serious negotiations begin). The main goal of these meetings is an establishment of personal contact, a clarification of interest, and achieving an agreement on further action (like a normal meeting in the office). Using the **registration list after a show** is also helpful. The only concern is that you do not have a trump card (to get in touch in advance) anymore, as after a conference many other providers will call, send e-mails, and prepare cheerful commercial proposals.

Exhibitors should use **every opportunity to collect the contact information of visitors**. First of all, the staff should be organized and efficient in their duties. They need to be instructed that their primary duty is **to speak to a great number of visitors** – not just to chat but to determine the need people have and to acquire their contact information. Each conversation should have four components: introduction of oneself and a company, understanding visitors' needs, acquiring visitors' contact information and agreeing on future steps. Some customers may require a lengthy conversation. Yes, it is definitely necessary to pay attention to them. However, do not miss out on the rest of them for one! There can be some precious leads there.

In addition, a booth enables contact information to be gathered without direct communication. For example, it is possible to hold **contests, competitions and quizzes**[13] where lead qualification issues may be included. In general, if you are out of time or lack ideas about contests, just give out souvenirs for business cards – it's better than nothing.

---

[13] Most organizers ask you to confirm with them any type of activity in order to be confident that it will not disturb other exhibitors. So make sure you have done this. Otherwise, your creative idea may just be nipped in the bud before it takes root and sprouts.

Organizers of events offer a range of marketing and advertising opportunities. Using some of them may bring new leads. These options may be included in a sponsorship package or sold separately. A good idea is to create a mailing about your products on behalf of the organizers well in advance of the event. Your letter should include a Call to Action, which inspires recipients to "show" themselves. The recipients should be encouraged to write you back, to follow a link, subscribe to a newsletter, or download some content, etc.

Another notable option is to **insert handouts in participants' bags**. These may be leaflets, feedback forms, or questionnaires that initiate some action on behalf of the clients. For example, a leaflet may ask a person to fill out a form, go to your booth, give it to your staff, and receive a "carrot." It is desirable to reward visitors with something visible to attract others, for example, give souvenirs in stylish shoulder bags. For B2B companies, a trial version of a product or free consulting can be offered. It is not as visible as other prizes, but will eventually bring leads of a higher quality.

I have not mentioned **speaking at events, banner placement or a logo on a ribbon**. Why? These things are mostly focused on creating a recognizable image of your company and they are hardly measurable in terms of new leads. You will never know who exactly of your customers has been influenced by brand advertising, except for the people who come to meet you on the spot. With these customers, everything is clear, but brand advertising is not so evident for those who may consider a purchase in future.

Another way is to **host your own event**. In terms of lead generation, this makes sense for products that have sales which include personal communication with a client. By the way, when you invite the target audience, you **inform more participants that those that actually register**, which makes it possible to identify interest in those leads who cannot come to event for some reason (e.g., due to the work overload, holidays, business trip, etc.).

Event Organization Main Actions

- Identify the target audience and lead qualification criteria.
- Organization and logistics: book a venue, rent equipment, order meals, print handouts, develop content and plan speakers, event web page, etc.
- Prepare a contact list.
- Choose a form of reporting on registrations (e.g., CRM).

- Prepare a call script, an e-mail and a questionnaire.
- PR and advertising support (if necessary).
- E-mail an invitation to an event.
- Active calling to gather registrations and find leads among those who are unable to come.
- Arrange one-on-one meetings at an event with the most interesting participants.
- Deliver follow-up calls and letters to find qualified leads after the event.
- Active sales.
- Transfer cold leads to the nurturing phase.
- Analyze results, calculate the conversion rate, ROI.

How do you **attract visitors of a desired level**? This is a key challenge when organizing hosted events. Free sandwiches are not a good teaser for C-level executives and managers – their time is too expensive. The main attractions are an **interesting program, keynote speakers, and exhibitors**. Most often, the personalities of speakers are more important than the themes of their speeches. When aiming for a hard-to-get audience, you should make the event more educational than advertisement. You need to "wrap up" your sales in this concept. For example, instead of having your own sales managers as speakers, ask one of your customers to speak. Instead of the name "Cosmetics of ABS Company" re-name the event "Youth recipes for those over 40." People are interested only in their own problems. Give them a chance to learn about the best practices when dealing with similar things!

Interesting content is only half the battle. You need to gather an audience, inform potential visitors about the exciting event, and invite them. The methods used to gather the audience for niche conferences are mostly **cold calls and direct mail**. If your event is of a wider scale, it makes sense to use **PR and brand advertising**. It may happen that you will manage to exchange information by partnering with some mass media, which results in publishing ads and putting online banners and announcements in event calendars. However, for highly specialized events, a loud PR can do harm to your campaign by attracting members of a non-target audience. Some event organizers warn that this is a private event and they have a right to refuse any registration. However, in practice, this policy is only followed when real free-riders try to visit a conference. However, even among the target audience, there are people who just love to go to events without buying anything or at least register for practically every conference. These members can bring down your performance on the final number of leads. However, it is not a good idea to refuse them, as it may damage your image. As they visit many events, they usually have lots of connections in professional circuits, so it is safer to host them as your most welcome guest. The most polite thing to do when dealing with them is to exclude them from future invitation lists.

The registration form may include more than contact information. Additionally, there may be questions **qualifying a delegate as a lead**. If you organize an event in a big city and you are inviting new potential customers, it is most likely that only about **50% of people registered will actually arrive**. If participants know about your company, not from hearsay, the number of attendees will be higher. Based on this concept, your list must include 60 people registered to have 30 participants coming to an event. To get 60 registrations, your invitation list to a target audience should include no fewer than 600 contacts (again, we are speaking about people who did not purchase from your company yet and are not loyal). Then, approximately 10% of them may be interested and register. Given that half of them do not attend an event (do not be upset – I have warned you! ☺), you will have 30 people attend. In smaller cities, a **turnout may fluctuate up to 70-80%**. In large cities, such a figure is a dream that can only be achieved in very exceptional cases. For example, we once gathered participants at **a conference about Apple business solutions hosted by an Apple partner**. It was a pure advertising event that promoted this partner. By tragic accident, it came a week after the death of Steve Jobs (RIP). It was decided to organize the event anyway, as business is business. Unexpectedly, almost all the registered delegated arrived; we even had to order additional meals. Clearly, this is quite an exceptional case and I really wish all the companies' heads long life and good health. However, I have not seen another example of a 100% turn-out of potential corporate clients of C-level, either for Apple products or for others, for a free event promoting one's services.

Getting back to the scheme of things: if you work with an outsourcing company to gather registrations, then after an event all contacts must be imported into your CRM system (if you make invitations on your own, it is definitely better to work in CRM from the very beginning) or organized with other of leads in another way that your company has adopted. You identify these leads' interests and start sales. To understand an **event's effectiveness** for the next time, it is essential to understand how many participants become your clients and how much the cost per lead is. Therefore, all the steps to closing a sale must be traceable and countable.

Webinars are becoming more common today instead of the traditional "offline" exhibitions. These are activities carried out over the Internet. They are good and have a low cost, although not as effective in terms of personal interaction. In addition, not all customers love visiting webinars. In general, for different target audiences, it makes sense to try different kinds of events. Then, you need to track the number of leads from them and make an overall conclusion on what should prevail in your marketing plan and in what order.

~~~ *Tip* ~~~
To improve turnout for webinars, it is recommended to give an additional reminder via phone to registered participants just 20 minutes before its start. Otherwise, on the very day, people may forget about it, being fascinated by something else (e.g., by one's work – why not?☺).
~~~

Events in general are an expensive activity, therefore, it is especially important to **estimate their effectiveness**. Here is an example of calculating the efficiency of an event. A VAR of communication equipment rented **a booth at a conference dedicated to wireless and mobile**. The conference was attended by about 800 people, but half of them were competitors, mass media, partners, etc. So the target group of customers included approximately 400 contacts. Managers working at a booth were able to speak to approximately 50 participants. Of these, 20 were qualified as leads. However, some of them were further excluded. It turned out that one of them had been already on board, another did not have a budget, and the third one used incompatible hardware.

At the same time, another marketer from this company used a **database of 1,500 contacts for telemarketing to appoint meetings**. This database contained C-level people of midsize companies. The call center started working on these companies. The purpose of the calls was to identify those who would need a communication system installation or upgrade in the next 12 months. As a result, 30 leads were identified and were transferred to the sales department. In the course of sales qualification, seven companies happened to not be ready for sales and went to the nurturing stage. For the 23 remaining leads, sales managers started setting up business meetings, doing negotiations, and preparing business proposals. In general, life began to boil.

Six months later, they summarized the results. Five customers identified via telemarketing and 10 found as a result of the conference have eventually bought hardware. The average amount of a sale was $60K. Of these, 30K was profit; the rest went to the cost of goods sold.

The following numbers resulted:

Parameter	Business meetings via telemarketing	A booth at the conference
Suspects (a database for telemarketing/participants invitation list)	1500 contacts	400 people
Leads	30	20
Qualified leads	23	17
Sales	5	10
Conversion	5/23 = 22%	10/17 = 59%
Income	$300,000	$600,000
Profit	$150,000	$300,000
Marketing expenses	$2,500	$12,000
Cost per lead	= 2,500/5=$500	=12,000/17=$706
ROI	(150,000 - 2 500)/ 2 500 = 59	(300 000 - 12 000)/12 000 = 24

In this table, the conversion rate, the cost per qualified lead, and the return on investment were crucial numbers. The **conversion rate** allowed marketers to evaluate the quality of leads. As we can see, for the event, the conversion rate was almost three times higher (22% and 59%). So it is clear from the data that the audience that had attended the conference was much more interested in data storage products. The audience became pre-selected participants based on the fact that they had already confirmed interest in the goods presented. However, the price of participation at a booth was rather high – $12,000. Therefore, the **cost per lead** happened to be 140% more expensive. A lead from the conference cost $706 and a lead received from a telemarketing was $500. **The ROI** was 24 for the event and 59 for the telemarketing, which means that a dollar spent on a marketing activity brought $24 or $59 of profit respectively.

In conclusion, I would like to warn you again. While **the cost of a lead may be high**, it does not always mean that this marketing tool should be excluded. It all depends on how many sales and leads you need to obtain in total. Some leads may cost more, some less – this is normal. Plus, maybe one particular marketing tool will someday outlive its effectiveness and then another will help.

Market Research for Gaining Leads

Market research **addressed to the right people that asks them the right questions** will help to reveal new leads and make new sales. The main thing is to formulate sufficient but not excessive questions. You can ask these people three or four questions, provide a form for getting contact information, and respect a respondent's wishes about how to be contacted.

For example, for one of our customers – a data storage systems vendor – we, **on behalf of an independent agency,** have completed **marketing research that assesses only two questions**. These questions were "What kind of data storage system does your company use now?" and "Are you planning to upgrade the system within a year?" We also asked the contacts of our respondent to send a ~~price~~ *prize* to the respondent for winning a lottery. The answers provided were sufficient for understanding the overall sales potential of the company.

The main problem with marketing surveys is that **people do not want to spend time answering questions**. In this regard, it is necessary to come up with a worthy motivation. When it comes to consumer goods, souvenirs (T-shirts, bags, toys) or an opportunity to win a valuable price in a draw can be awarded for a questionnaire filled in. For corporate sales, the best motivation is the one that brings any business benefits, for example, one hour of free consulting (you can limit them to three per week, for example, not to become a charity organization), valuable content, free tickets to an upcoming business show or some benefits related to your product. Thus, participation in your market research becomes a business task for your potential customer and thus it may be included in a daily routine.

As always in lead generation, the most important thing about marketing research is to get as many of the questionnaires of the "right" people as possible. To do this, your target group needs to be informed about ongoing research and be invited to participate. The **range of tools for attracting an audience is wide enough** – mailings, announcements on social networks, advertisements in relevant resources, etc. You can also use cold calls if anticipated income makes these investments sensible.

The most convenient way to analyze research results is by using **marketing survey software**. It saves time by conducting data processing for you and it minimizes errors. There are cloud software services for running marketing research. (They do not require installation on your computer and are available through your browser.) For small surveys, you can use some of them for free.

As a result of conducting marketing research with the purpose of lead generation, you will gain **contacts of potential buyers and additional qualifying information**. Perhaps, some respondents will indicate that they do not want to receive additional information from you. Well, if so, you can try to contact them personally "from zero," not following a survey, to arrange a business meeting.

Main Actions for Conducting Market Research

- Identify the target audience and lead qualification criteria.
- Prepare a contact list and/or a list of target resources for PR.
- Choose a form of reporting (e.g., CRM).
- Prepare a questionnaire (plus a call script and an e-mail if you use telemarketing and e-mail marketing).
- If calling is planned: test a call script on a small sample and correct it.
- Gather answers.
- Lead qualification and scoring.
- Active sales.
- Transfer cold leads to the nurturing phase.
- Analyze results, calculate the conversion.

A pleasant **side effect** of market research is data about the use of your products among its target audience (or other issues that you think need to be clarified). Drawing upon these data points, an analytical report can be prepared. In the future, this report can be downloaded on a website (of course, after getting one's contacts☺) or published in specialized mass media.

E-mail Marketing to Encourage Action

The **reputation of e-mails as a marketing tool** is often tainted by lots of spam that pours into our inboxes. However, the effectiveness of a properly compiled letter sent to the right target audience is very high, especially considering the minimal financial and time expenditure. A personalized e-mail differs from spam, as it is sent to a specific person and is related to his or her interests. The **source where you got an e-mail must be legal** for the country in which you operate. Finally, a letter should identify the **sender, providing one's name and title, direct contacts with an office, cell phone, e-mail, and URL.**

A good e-mail letter can carry out a **wide range of tasks**. It can help you to make a sale, agree on a business meeting, confirm participation in an event, and acquire answers to market research. E-mails are widely used in nurturing potential buyers. For this, most e-mail marketing systems provide the functionality of sending a series of messages with a certain time interval that depends on a person's actions. E-mails are used everywhere in lead generation, so I shall dedicate a separate chapter to them. Now, let's talk about the process of sending out lead generation e-mails and measuring their results.

E-mail marketing has excellent opportunities for **testing**. For each e-mail, it is recommended to make a separate landing (in landing page generators, a process of making a copy of an already existing landing takes seconds) to track clicks and measure results. During testing, you can easily make changes and see the result: you can update text, letter layout, and subject. You can look at the reactions of your customers. It's amazing how these changes can work wonders!

By the way, your product category has its **best time for e-mailing.** The best time is the time when your customers have a greater possibility of opening and reading a letter. What time is it? I don't know – this should be tested. For recreation and entertainment goods and services, this is probably a weekend or an evening. For corporate business, it is advisable to send e-mails during working hours. First, a letter has more chance not to be deleted together with overnight spam. Second, e-mails from new senders received after 7 p.m. look suspicious; if a sender's company cannot plan the working hours of its employees so that they can finish their business before the end of a working day, will the project or delivery of goods for a customer be completed on time?

In regard to the **quantitative results of e-mailing**, the two most important things are the number of **e-mails opened** and the clicks on links within a letter: **click-through-rate** or CTR. CTR is calculated as the percentage of recipients that clicked on a link out of the total number of recipients. It is also used as a metric for measuring results of any online advertising. All e-mail marketing software systems suggest CTR analysis and some of them even allow comparison with an average CTR for your sphere of business. For example, according to MailChimp, the average percentage of openings for e-mails devoted to vitamin supplements is 17.27% and the average CTR is 1.98%, while for home and garden topics, the average percentage is 25.05% and the average CTR is 3.93%[14].

However, CTR is just an intermediate result. The ultimate goal is **attaining leads**. In the case of e-mail software integration with a CRM, the amount of routine work devoted to copying responses will be kept to a minimum. For new leads, there should be an indication of their source. Thus, the status of all the contacts can be tracked further: what sales are closed, which leads are being negotiated, which have refused, etc.

The effectiveness of e-mailing is influenced by three factors:
- the contact list by which a message is sent;
- its content;
- its format and layout.

By having an ideal combination of these three components, you'll get the maximum number of responses. The **contact list you use for mailings** should be up to date. This list should match your target audience and contain as many direct e-mails as possible. The data may be received in different ways. For example, they can be bought from business data providers, gathered at a show, or collected via your website.

Let's look at an **example**: a company providing marketing software was participating in a conference for chief marketing officers, marketing directors, and marketing managers. They were focused on making contacts with as many suspects as possible and establishing long-term relationships with existing customers. At their booth they installed a touch screen for submitting contacts to participate in a draw for a travel certificate worth 1000 euros. After two days at the show, they received 400 people's contact information. Was it expensive or not? A sponsorship package including a contact list would cost up to 10 times more, excluding expenses for a booth and additional costs of participation. As a result, all the contacts received were added to a list of recipients for the company's lead nurturing newsletter.

The text of a letter should include an introduction of you and your company, the main idea of your proposal, and **a call to action** that you want the addressee to do. For example, if we need people to fill in an online questionnaire, we encourage them to click on a link and complete this before a deadline to get a gift or discount. When trying to arrange a business meeting, I suggest an exact time. The average buyer does not have time to think hard about what to do next. It is essential to provide simple questions and calls to action.

---

[14] Source: MailChimp E-mail Marketing Benchmarks:
http://mailchimp.com/resources/research/email-marketing-benchmarks/ (December, 2015)

~~~ *Tip* ~~~
Use postscripts to get more attention from your addressees. Today, when people mostly read texts with many links (and not a good old newspaper, for example) for many of them, it is hard to read a text line by line. People tend to jump to the most important information. So use postscripts to generalize the main information and to ask once again what you want.
PS. Even if your attendee has read the whole letter from the very beginning, postscripts will increase the number of responses and a CTR.
Test it and you'll see!
~~~

If we talk about the **format of a letter**, it depends on the goal of a letter, the kind of business, and even on the region of the recipient. For example, when arranging business meetings, the format of personal letters works best. Such letters should not look like an advertisement or a mass mailing. They do not need a variety of fonts or any pictures. However, for the same target audience, an invitation to an event may have pictures and a colorful layout. The proportion of the text and pictures I recommend is maximum 70/30. But anyway, my experience shows that the simpler the letter the better. Make it as short as possible; from the first paragraph it should be clear what you want.

Main Actions for E-mailing

- Identify the target audience and lead qualification criteria.
- Prepare a contact list.
- Prepare the text of a letter and a landing.
- Choose a form of reporting (e.g., CRM).
- Mail a small sample for testing.
- Correct the text.
- Mail.
- Gather leads, their qualification and scoring.
- Active sales.
- Transfer cold leads to the nurturing phase.
- Analyze results, calculate the conversion rate and ROI.

Snail Mail for Lead Generation

There is a rare category of potential customers for whom "offline" letters work better than any other means of communication. The first group includes buyers that cannot be easily reached by phone or e-mail. Perhaps you just do not have their direct contact information or cannot get any response although you have tried several times. Mailings are respected by old school people for whom paper is significant. Is this your client? I don't know. **Testing will tell.** Try to mail a few small samples. Based on this, you will make a conclusion about the usefulness of this method. When sending mail, it is important not to have your document go into the trash. When people receive mail, they first look at its appearance. Reputable letters attract attention – it's human nature. Cheap flyers will also work, especially for a mass market, such as a pizza delivery or sanitary engineering services. Their price is quite low, so the flyers can be quickly spread on a geographical basis. When it comes to services that require **reliability and reputation** (e.g., banking, car dealers, yacht club, etc.), a letter should look presentable and mimic a very **valuable document**. Such correspondence is often sent in a large envelope with thick paper. A paper postal packet also looks awesome. The envelope can read VIP or Urgent – let these words inspire those who accompany a letter in its journey. In short, a letter should serve to inspire its addressee to open it.

Once the letter is opened, **its content** can be serious or funny, emotional or calm. It depends on the specifics of products sold and the target audience. It is important to have a simple understanding about who the product or service is representing and how it can be contacted. It should also be clear when it is necessary to make a decision and why it's better to do this as soon as possible. The most important thing here again is a **call to action that provides an opportunity to track leads**. The specifics of postal deadlines for answering or doing some action cannot be too strict. Therefore, a call to action must be both stimulating and diplomatic. For example, in corporate sales, you can propose a business meeting for a certain date, but at the same time in a postscript, please add that these dates are flexible and you can wait for another proposal if they are not fine about it. Or, you can to invite them to register at an event in advance to ensure the availability of tickets. The main thing is that people should show themselves and have outlined their interest or a lack of it.

Most letters to C-level are usually checked by **a secretary or a personal assistant** before going to a top manager. Therefore, it is important to pass through this barrier. To do this, the text of a letter should be written in such a way that a secretary will be persuaded to deem it important and personalized. There are a few things which may help: personal appeal ("Dear Harrison"), company brand information like a logo and a letterhead, a number and a date of outgoing correspondence (if it is common in your sphere), a signature by hand, your personal contact details with a mobile phone number – all this depending on the business communication style that is used in your industry.

At the same time, it will be great if a letter creates an impression that a sender knows the addressee in person. This effect can be achieved by the following methods: "Unfortunately, I could not reach you on the phone, so I am sending a personal letter," or "As intended, I am sending you this information..." What? Is this on the verge of ethics? Yes, but it works! But, please do not overplay with a level of personalization and do not make false statements. For example, it will spoil your impression if you write something like "as we agreed" or "following our conversation" and you did not have any such agreement or conversation.

Mailings for consumer market promotion can be addressed to a wide mass of people even without a name. However, if you have a list of people who have previously provided their contact information with permission to send them proposals, bulk snail mail may be effective to move them through the sales cycle.

Main actions for postal mailings

- Identify the target audience and lead qualification criteria.
- Prepare a contact list.
- Choose a form of reporting (e.g., CRM).
- Prepare a letter/flyer: a text and design (if necessary).
- Print letters or flyers (or several variants).
- Test several variants of letters and flyers (if possible).
- Mail.
- Gather leads, their qualification and scoring.
- Active sales.
- Transfer cold leads to the nurturing phase.
- Analyze results; calculate the conversion rate and ROI.

Bulk "offline" mailing is definitely more expensive than e-mailing. Its cost depends on a level of **personalization in a letter, on its look,** and the postal method. It is true that all elements can be completed by your marketing or administrative department by themselves, but this is a huge amount of a routine work which is better to outsource to a mailing company that runs these processes in the most optimal way.

The most reliable and fast delivery is by **express courier**. But it does not make sense for low-cost products: a price of one express delivery even in a mass order is up to $6, and $2-3 more will be spent for the preparation of a letter itself. Express courier delivery does not always make sense for B2B products as well; a courier is usually met by a secretary and all the pomp and circumstance mean nothing. Such a case occurred for one company when they wanted to invite the top level of large corporations to their event and hired beautiful fashion models as couriers. They were dressed in beautiful costumes and looked amazing. But the problem was that the models were not allowed to reach the decision maker. The secretary and the security simply did not allow them to enter. What a waste of money!

The results of postal mailings or flyer distribution are not easy to trace. But don't give up! You can specify a **different phone number** with a counter of incoming calls (it can readdress calls to your normal phone and serve just for counting). However, it is clear that if someone comes to your corporate website and calls the number indicated on it, you will hardly understand the source of this lead. After all, you don't want to conduct an extreme interrogation.

If a customer is expected to answer you by post as well, you can insert in a letter a prepared envelope with your return address and an order form. The general rule for measuring results is the same as for all other types of lead generation: **count all leads, peel apart unqualified ones, see how qualified leads turn into sales, and calculate profit and ROI.** Even if you make a few errors about the number of leads, it is important to track large sales. On this basis, the effectiveness of mailing for sales growth can be estimated.

Mailing Mass Media Subscribers

In every industry, there is a certain number of **well-known reliable mass media and online information channels** from which people receive regular newsletters. You can consider cooperation with event agencies that specialize in your industry, which also have large relevant contact lists. An advantage of using these external channels is the ability to **get new leads quickly** and **save time,** as you do not need to build a contact list. However, a drawback is that you just rent a list and do not own it, so you can use it only for the number of times for which you pay.

When selecting mass media, first of all one needs to estimate the audience's demographics to see if it includes the target group and in what quantity. You also need to understand how your message will be sent – either individually or among others (and, if so, in what sequence).

Your message will be sent by a third party on your behalf. In this correspondence, this method cannot be personal and is not suitable for arranging meetings and conference calls. However, mailings to mass media lists are very effective to **invite attendees to events, announce market research, and encourage customers through discounts, if this applies to your goods**. A lead generation message must focus on appeal so that a person can "show" him or herself by calling, writing a response, clicking a link, or conducting actions on a landing page prior to a deadline. The reason why a prospect buyer should start to seize the opportunity should be reasonably justified. For example, there are only 10 prizes or a limited number of tickets for a tasting evening.

A **landing page** that is referred to within a letter must describe your proposal in terms of its key benefits, and request contact details of visitors, promising them some bonus for this information, such as a free version of market research, a white paper, or a discount. Landing pages generating software allow all requests from any number of pages to be stored in a single database. It is also necessary to receive notifications about each request by e-mail, to take into account the most valuable opportunities immediately.

The following numbers should be **measured** in regards to a newsletter: the number of clicks by links provided, the number of leads, and qualified leads. These leads are moved to active sales, and, as a result, it is possible to estimate the final return on investment.

Main Actions for Mass Media Subscribers' Mail

- Choose a mass media or an online channel.
- Negotiate and contract.
- Create a letter and a landing.
- Mail control.
- Gather leads and their qualification.
- Import leads to CRM.
- Active sales.
- Transfer cold leads to the nurturing phase.

- Analyze results, calculate the conversion rate and ROI.

An Undiscovered Potential of SMS Marketing

SMS advertising seems annoying to many people and I am not an exception. However, a good point about this specific niche from a marketing point of view is that a person is forced to view the message – at least out of the corner of their eye, even if it happens when deleting the text.

Advantages of SMS marketing are as follows: a **high percentage of opening and reading, a wide spread of cell phones, and a low cost**. A mobile phone is convenient, as a person almost always has it within arm's reach, and most cell phones' standard settings presume that SMS notifications are coming directly to a main screen.

A drawback of SMS is that they are short (in most countries up to 160 characters) and that by the laws of most countries you are **not allowed to send bulk SMS to unknown recipients.** You can send them only to those who have agreed to receive them from you. In the USA, for example, you need to have a written consent from a person to send SMS. Otherwise, an SMS will be considered spam, which carries a fee of up to $1,500.

In marketing, SMS are most often used to **inform existing customers about promotions and news**, as well as for **lead nurturing** (mostly for a mass market). They are very popular among retailers which provide constant discounts and promotions. These retailers also inform their buyers about them. For example, a car dealer informs its customers about an offer to trade in an old car for a new one using some special conditions. A beauty salon sends invitations to buy LPG massage with 50% discount. The main thing is that invitations should be sent only to addressees who have agreed to receive information.

But cheer up, my reader! **Not everything is lost in terms of lead generation** via SMS. The main thing is to follow the law. For example, an agreement to receive SMS can be achieved when participating in large industry shows and expos. Turn on your fantasy! And let me give you more examples to inspire you.

You may be prohibited to send SMS to new recipients, but you are definitely allowed to **receive them.** SMS marketing may help a buyer to **notify a vendor about his or her interest in a service**. I would not recommend SMS as the only means of dealing with a target audience, but for some of your potential customers it may work. For example, a travelling service agency published an advertisement with the following words: "Send a free SMS to 12345 with the text 'I love sun' and we shall offer you the best ideas about winter vacations at the best sea and ocean sunny beaches of Asia." After receiving an SMS, the manager of an agency comes in contact with those who are dreaming about tanned skin, clarifies their wishes and requirements, and invites them to an office to discuss unique options.

Here is another example from **a B2B market**. At a professional conference, a speaker announces a release of a product and describes its awesome features. The audience is impressed! At the end of a speech, the speaker shows a slide: "To get a free demo, please send an SMS to 54321." While the speaker keeps the attention of the audience, there is a strong chance that he or she will receive respondents. In answer to the SMS, access to a free version is sent. Of course, there will remain people who prefer to go to a booth or to a website, make a profound choice by themselves, and disregard possible free options and discounts. However, you can always get more leads by using various means of communications, and SMS is only one of them.

Main Actions for SMS Marketing

- Choose a service provider for SMS mailing.
- Prepare a contact list (if applicable).
- Test.
- SMS mailing.
- Gather leads, their qualification and scoring.
- Import leads to CRM.
- Active sales.
- Transfer cold leads to the nurturing phase.
- Analyze results, calculate the conversion rate and ROI.

A Corporate Website as a Trap for Leads

A corporate website may be visited by a large number of potential buyers who you will never know anything about. They do not show themselves. They just try to find some information and after they find it, or not – they are gone. It is not clear what these visitors were concerned with, what they were looking for, why they left, or if they went to your competitor's site. But these visitors could have been one step from asking information about or buying your product. What a shame to lose them! Therefore, the lead generation mission of a website is **not to miss potential buyers** and to give them every opportunity to **show themselves**. If you use a few simple rules, you can get a larger number of contacts of people interested in your products and services. The main goal is to collect as many contacts as possible, see if there are leads among them, and take them into the sales process.

First of all, a website should be easy to find for potential customers; it should be **indexed in a search engine**, depending on your ambitions, in the first lines or pages of results. Search engine optimization is a topic about which there has already been lots of attention provided by other authors, so I shall not get into details. Rather, let's discuss what happens when a person visits your website.

A website should look attractive. However, I am mostly concerned about its **effectiveness in terms of lead generation and sales rather than creativity**. Sometimes, it happens that the most successful websites in terms of selling are quite modest in design. Looks do not matter if the site performs its lead generation function and brings contact information of visitors that have some probability of turning into customers. According to an Acsend2[15] survey, website owners understand this, and the main objective of a website is to increase lead generation.

---

[15] Ascend2, Website Marketing Optimization Benchmark Summary Report, 2014. www.ascend2.com

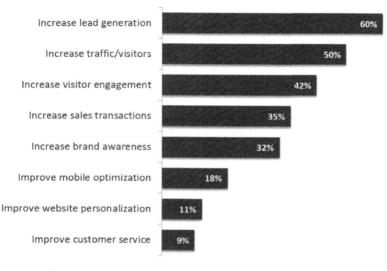

Pic.13. The most important objectives for a website for a year ahead
Source: Ascend2, Website Marketing Optimization Benchmark Summary Report

Each page of a website should encourage a visitor **to perform some action**. When you create a new page, ask yourself: "What do I want people to do?" Attract visitors' attention to these actions and tell them what is expected from them: "download," "click," or "register." A site provides broad opportunities for experimenting with different types of **"carrots" for buyers** to show themselves. These include bonuses, gifts, "2 for 1" promotions, discounts, prize draws, etc. Specify **deadlines** ("A discount is valid until March 15!") and explain why a person should **react quickly** ("There are only 7 seats left!"). All this should encourage people to make a decision sooner than if they would "mature" by themselves. Test new pages and new stimuli. By doing testing, you will be able to choose the kind of motivation that works best for your customer.

It is necessary to enable potential customers to contact you in **all the ways that you are able to maintain** such as telephone, e-mail, feedback forms, and Skype – all of them can bring new contacts of potential buyers, who, for some reason, are more comfortable with this or that means of communication. Of course, companies today are adding to their website social network plugins and integration with Facebook, Twitter, YouTube, and LinkedIn. It may be essential to add a plugin for **online chat** with visitors. And – sure, otherwise all efforts are in vain, you should provide its operational support.

Publishing **valuable information** that is available for **download** after filling out a contact form and answering a couple of qualification questions is a good example of lead generation via a website. The website may include the following materials: **educational brochures, marketing surveys, analytics, white papers, video, presentations, and books**. Preparation of this unique content is a time-consuming process for a marketing department. However, it is a long-term investment that will work for a significant amount of time. Thus, your site will be able to gather leads and do the first level of qualification. However, if you care about a customer, do not overload the contact form with too many questions. It is better to clarify some details a bit later then to frighten your prospects now.

Pekka Huttunen, CEO for Liana Technologies, a Finnish-based company specializing in digital marketing and communication software, provides the following **example**: "The most effective channel for lead generation for our company was an educational book about e-mail marketing which we have released. Our 'E-mail marketing guide book' was downloaded more than 7000 times. The book is a collection of practical tips for achieving the desired results from e-mail marketing. It is free access but to get it you need to fill out a contact form and opt for subscribing to a company newsletter." [16]

Another option is a **subscription to company's newsletter**. This will collect the contacts of people interested in your company, in your products, or just in your specialization. However, not all the contacts gathered like this will be treated as leads. These can be partners, journalists, analysts, and potential employees.

Website Lead Generation Opportunities

- Request contacts when downloading educational materials, marketing surveys, analytics, white papers, video, presentations, and books.
- Provide a wide range of communication means to come in contact with your company.
- Use feedback forms and "Ask an expert."
- Provide calls to action: "download," "click," "read," "register" and ask to do this NOW, because...
- Provide a subscription to newsletters.
- Offer a live online chat with your managers.

---

[16] Liana Technologies provided this case study (www.lianatech.com)

- Use pop-up windows which appear after some time on the website proposing, e.g., to call you back in 26 seconds.
- Invite to your company's events.

You can also start from the end. Your ultimate goal is to get contacts of potential customers, isn't it? Ok! When people visit your website, **ask for their contact details** and a couple of qualification questions (city, age, gender). This is what MyHabit does, an online designer discount retailer run by Amazon.com. MyHabit positions themselves as a discounter for a selected audience, which explains why they start with asking for contact information. Regardless, some variation of this approach may work even for the B2B market.

As always, all the leads need to be **imported into CRM** to see their conversion rate. This will allow you to evaluate the website's lead generation tools and make a calculation of its efficiency. The best thing to reduce the amount of mechanical work is to integrate a website and CRM or to use marketing automation software specially designed to track online leads and display their activity on a website.

Search Engine Advertising

Lead generation on the Net is worthy of a separate book. Its significant part would be devoted to advertising in search engines. The most popular search engine is **Google, which occupies about 70% share** of this market (by September of 2015)[17]. But in some countries, Google is not a winner of people's choice award: Yahoo is extremely popular in Japan and Taiwan, Yandex is more widespread in Russia, and Naver in South Korea.

The main feature of our digital data era is that almost all information is available on the Net. Therefore, a buyer can find everything he or she needs to make a decision and can be very well self-prepared when approaching a seller. As a result, you need **to find a potential customer not only ready to buy, but also at a stage of searching for information**. And here search engine advertising helps greatly.

Advertising in search engines is widely used for **mass market** goods such as clothes, electronics, accessories, kids' goods, banks and

---

[17] Source: https://www.netmarketshare.com/search-engine-market-share.aspx?qprid=4&qpcustomd=0

insurance companies, education, auto dealers, and real estate. Most often, a decision to purchase these products is made in a rather short period of time. Search engine advertising is used for **B2B sales.** Landing pages for products with a long purchase cycle usually include some valuable information to encourage a visitor to leave contact information, which may include white papers, analytics reports, demos, or other possibilities to receive something for free.

However, the main reason for trying search engine advertising for immediate lead generation effect is not about the business sector. It does not matter whether it is a mass market or B2B. In both cases, there are examples of successes and epic failures. The key thing to take into consideration is whether **there is demand for your products in the Net or not**. I mean: if your products are innovative and nobody looks for anything similar in Google, you will be unable to get qualified hot leads from a search engine. Even if you chose key words that are close to your product idea, most of your customers will need to be nurtured first or persuaded that although the product is a new one, it has excellent feedback and they can rely on the supplier's reputation. Even if a market is immature, search engines can give you contacts of prospective customers, but the path to them will be longer and may be more expensive. You will need to educate your target audience about your products at the same time as doing lead generation. Then people will start searching for your products more and more, and search engines will bring you more qualified leads.

Even if you **hire an Internet advertising agency** to run your campaigns on Google and on other resources, it helps to understand the main principles of search engine advertising when one receives reports from an agency and tries to understand what is going on. Some agencies work for a percentage of your advertising budget and thus they may not be interested in making costs lower. You see, I am quite cost-conscious about your marketing budget☺. So let's discuss the main principles of making advertising so that it will bring the maximum leads at the lowest price.

Search engine ads are shown to a user **in accordance with a search request.** They are located above search results in the upper position, down position, and as a left or right side banner, which may or may not include a picture. As the content coincides (at least, should somehow coincide) with a user's search request, they are taken positively and sometimes even not treated as advertising.

Advertising in search engines is **available for every budget**. Its principle is the following: advertisers determine a budget and a cost up to which they can pay per click (cost per click or CPC) on their ad by their target group. On a basic level, it is like an auction where an advertiser paying more gets more demonstrations of an ad. An advertiser pays per click. (However, there are options like paying for a thousand demonstrations, but they are not as effective.) A search engine's algorithm first of all automatically chooses the most expensive bids, and then as soon as they are "finished" (in terms of limits set by their advertisers), the search engine shows cheaper bids. So if you have a small budget, you have a chance to be shown, possibly less frequently and at a lower position. Maybe if you have set too low a price for too wide a target group, your ads may never be shown. If you narrow the target group (for example, choose not all the USA but only some states), the average CPC will also slow down. So if the frequency of your ad demonstrations and your position does not suit you – raise the budget or change the target group and you'll get more. Another factor that influences the frequency of showing your ads is Google's quality score. This is a metric determining, generally speaking, an ad's popularity and its relevance to a user. It is based on the number of clicks per ad and its landing content. The idea of scoring ads is that for Google it is more profitable to show less expensive ads with better CTR than more expensive ones that never get clicked (as they will earn less on them). A win-win situation for both an advertiser with a high CPC and the search engine!

The most important thing to remember is that the effectiveness of ads should be **determined not by the number of clicks** (however, this is what you pay to a search engine for), **but by the number of leads and the ROI on them**. Search engines provide instruments to evaluate the number of leads that have clicked your ad, followed to a landing, and carried out some action required there (visited some page or clicked on some button). This is called a **conversion tracking** tool, and, with its help, Google allows tracking downloads, sign-ups, clicks on links or buttons, and even calls by a phone number.

The **general strategy of the lead generation process utilizing search engines is the following**. An advertiser chooses a target audience by region, language, gender, age, etc. For example, if you provide cell phone services in Spain, you do not need to promote your company in the rest of the world. The narrower the group, the cheaper the average cost per click is. Then an advertiser creates a campaign and indicates keywords, text of the advertisements, and links to web pages. One may also choose whether to do ads only on specific search engines or also on its partner websites where the relevant target audience will find it. (However, I recommend running these campaigns separately to see their effectiveness compared.) After that, it takes some time (usually about a day) for a search engine team to approve your campaign. When a person clicks on advertisements, he or she is transferred to a website or a **landing page** created for this campaign. It is important to **track all the leads** coming from a concrete ad so you can optimize your campaign and use the most effective text. Search engine analytics provide wide opportunities for this. Without tracking leads, you may just achieve a brand awareness effect, or at least not reach the maximum of your lead generation potential.

The key factors that influence the success of a search engine advertising campaign are the following:
- an existing demand for your products on the Net;
- competitors that can "overbid" your ads;
- keywords selected;
- the text of advertisements;
- a landing page.

A **demand** is the current state of affairs. This may be changed by a prolonged advertising campaign, together with PR and brand advertising. However, it takes time, and, in this case, advertising on search engines will not give an immediate effect. **High competition** should not make you afraid. It is generally good if your competitors use this lead generation method actively, as it is likely that they have already tested it and it provided good leads. However, this advertising battle may require a decent budget. As for advertisements' keywords, the text, and the landing – all these things are a subject for constant testing to see the most effective variants that provide the best results.

The process of creating **a set of keywords** can be significantly efficient in regards to time management by using the appropriate services that suggest keywords similar to those which you have initially chosen. Google offers Keyword Planner, which gives ideas on additional keywords and provides statistics on their popularity. Definitely, popularity influences price: the more popular – the more expensive. It would be more effective for a budget to choose lots of narrowed keywords. The total number of keywords may by up to several hundred and even in the thousands. Some of these words will bring more qualified leads, some less, and some may bring nothing. It is a matter of testing to find a balance between the desired number of qualified leads and a reasonable amount of clicks and their price.

The **text** of an ad informs a prospective buyer about an offer and provides a call to action; it also states a reason why a person should click on it immediately. The length of a text has limits, so it is a genuine art to create laconic, powerful, and, at the same time, grammatically correct text. In Google AdWords, ad titles are limited to 25 characters and the two description lines are limited to 35 characters each. A display URL is up to 35 characters. Ideally, a text should not only be short and strong but also include keywords searched by a prospective buyer. This increases the chances that a person will click on an ad. However, I have to direct your attention once to the following: the number of clicks is not a key goal. If a person clicks on an extremely attractive ad and then bounces to a landing that does not support the sweet promises of an ad – an advertiser loses money.

On a **landing page,** there should be information about your products and their benefits, customers' feedback, an order form, your contacts, online chat, etc. Some products can be sold online immediately, but, even for them, it is important to gather contacts of those who are not ready to buy now and need to be nurtured. Visitors should be encouraged to leave their contacts so you can begin some interaction with them. I emphasize that the **speed and quality of processing requests** is very important.

Landings should **be tested as well for their titles, pictures, and calls to action**. It is normal to have several landings for different target groups. It is better to create a sample that can be edited by marketing people without the need to involve a programmer or designer. Landing page generators offering user friendly services of creation may also help to speed up this process without the need to develop everything from scratch.

Search engines provide a great opportunity to **manage an advertising process in real time** and provide **powerful analytical tools**. Google Analytics provides various opportunities for a comparative analysis of different campaigns and helps to choose the most effective instruments for lead generation. In general, advertising in search engines provides **room for maneuvering** in terms of costs and results, obtains leads which can be taken into the sales process, and increases the profit of your business.

In conclusion, search engine advertising theory contains one more important tidbit. Literally speaking, **your testing will last as long as your advertising campaign runs**. Yes, there will be a beginning when testing occupies 100% of your work. Later, you will need to check the conversion of clicks to leads, work with analytics, track closed sales, and make all the adjustments you can to improve the number and the quality of leads. Of course, there will be periods when no adjustments are necessary, as everything is running smoothly. But anyway, every online advertisement needs **constant control,** as the **online environment changes very quickly.** For example, the arrival of new advertisers promoting the same keywords may change your statistics, even though all your settings remain the same. You will need to make new edits to get the same results.

Search engine advertising main steps

- Define the target audience.
- Define the keywords.
- Prepare ads (text, image).
- Create landings.
- Add conversion tracking tools to landings.
- Test keywords, ads, landings.
- Campaign launch.
- Constantly check campaign results and analytics; make improvements if necessary.
- Identify leads, their qualification and scoring.
- Sales active phase.
- Transfer cold leads to the nurturing phase.
- Analyzing results, calculate the conversion rate and ROI.

Let's have a look at an example. AGAT, one of **Hyundai's partners,** a large automotive dealer with more than 5,000 employees, was investigating new lead generation opportunities[18]. Previously, the auto dealer had used mostly brand advertising on outdoor banners, ads in glossy magazines, and publications in a business press. All sales were made in car showrooms. The company had decided to test Internet lead generation and hired an agency that specialized in lead generation. This lead generation campaign's goal was to acquire **requests from prospective buyers who wished to receive a proposal about purchasing a new car.**

A set of **landing pages** was created. Navigating from search engines and other Internet resources, a user was suggested the best offer for a new car. It is curious that testing showed that **non-branded pages worked better** than branded landings that had a logo, mentioned the company, or its slogan. The non-branded pages gave more leads. The campaign achieved a conversion rate of 2.8%. Out of 1000 clicks, 28 people completed an application to receive an offer. This conversion rate

---

[18] AGAT Group and E-Promo provided this case study (http://agat-group.com, http://www.e-promo.ru)

was nearly two times higher than the conversion rate for branded landing pages, which was only 1.5%. In addition, non-branded pages were simpler in terms of design and could be generated faster. Lead generation specialists **tested different versions of text and changed the application** to acquire a formula that performed at peak demand. Through this process, the agency was able to increase the number of visits converting into applications and work with various traffic sources effectively.

Here are the results achieved after three months of the campaign:

Parameter	Internet lead generation for a car dealer
Cost per lead (all website applications)	$31
Cost per qualified lead (a lead which has agreed to meet in a car showroom to view a sales offer or undergo calculation of credit)	$48
Conversion of visitors into leads	2.8%
Income/marketing expenses[19]	166

All the leads received as a result of this campaign were managed in **CRM**, which the auto dealer's marketing managers, sales managers, and showroom directors used. This allowed the company to estimate the effectiveness of further sales work done on leads received. However, the company discovered that initially **sales managers lacked experience** in this aspect of communication, which during the first stage lowered the percentage of deals closed. Training fixed this problem, and, as the sales managers gained experience, sales conversion increased.

This project demonstrated that **Internet lead generation provided good results for the auto dealer.** Lead generation was economically rational and could be improved when every department worked on efficiently.

---

[19] In this example we see that the auto dealer operates with total income but not with profit, as an indicator for calculating the effectiveness of a marketing campaign. So I do not use the term ROI in the sense that I use it in the rest of the book.

Leads from Social Networks

Good news for advertisers! Social networking now occupies almost 30% of our daily Internet activities[20]. In 2015, the average user spent 1.77 hours per day on social platforms. That is where leads can be caught! The champions are Thailand, Argentina, Malaysia, Qatar, Mexico, and South Africa where people check social media applications at least 40 times a day[21].

The market leader is Facebook. It has surpassed 1.59 billion registered accounts as of the fourth quarter of 2015[22]. YouTube has over a billion users – almost one-third of all people on the Internet[23]. There have been lots of debates about Google+ recently, as its number of active users is significantly less than the huge army of all the Google users. In October 2014, Google+ boss Dave Besbris rather pointedly said: "I don't want to talk about numbers,"[24] but there are people who want to talk about them☺. Kevin Anderson, an analytics and visualization blogger, thinks that just 9% of its users actively post public content.[25]

Social Network Platforms	Number of Active Users per Month (4rd quarter of 2015)
Facebook	1.59 billion
YouTube	1 billion
Instagram	650 million[26]
LinkedIn	414 million
Twitter	305 million
Google+	198 million (estimated)
Pinterest	176 million [27]

Number of users per social network by the end of 2015
Sources: www.statista.com, www.digitaltrends.com, www.expandedramblings.com

---

[20] GlobalWebIndex reports on the latest trends in social networking. Free summary: http://insight.globalwebindex.net/social
[21] DigitalTrends.com: http://www.digitaltrends.com/mobile/informate-report-social-media-smartphone-use/
[22] Statista, Facebook: number of monthly active users worldwide: http://www.statista.com/statistics/264810/number-of-monthly-active-facebook-users-worldwide/
[23] YouTube official statistics: https://www.youtube.com/yt/press/statistics.html
[24] http://recode.net/2014/10/07/new-google-head-david-besbris-were-here-for-the-long-haul-qa/
[25] https://ello.co/dredmorbius/post/nAya9WqdemIoVuVWVOYQUQ
[26] http://www.digitaltrends.com/social-media/instagram-is-rapidly-increasing-the-number-of-ads-users-see/
[27] http://expandedramblings.com/index.php/pinterest-stats/

Social network users are eager to **share personal information** so advertisers can easily find their potential buyers. The main difference between advertising in search engines and in social networks is that on Google a **user takes some action like searching keywords** and thus "reveals" oneself, while **on social network sites, the advertising is targeted by a user's profile**. Here is the main reason why one method should not exclude the other. Instead, these two methods should work in conjunction. It will allow you to gather all of the reachable leads on the Net. Social network advertisements are shown to users if they fit the profile of a target audience of an advertiser by age, gender, education, marital status; country, city, district, metro station, streets; school, faculty, school, year of higher education; position (if specified); interests and hobbies, etc. Business social networks allow limiting an audience by professional performance, such as industry, position, competence, business scale, company size, etc.

Popular social media sites offer **different ways to advertise brands**. Facebook offers advertisers use of promoted posts, sponsored stories, page post ads, external website ads, etc. On Twitter, there are promoted tweets and accounts that show up on users' newsfeeds. On YouTube, you can promote a video or a channel, or use advertising played before or inserted into a video. Advertising formats vary greatly from one social network to another and may change with every system update. The general idea is the same as for every online lead generation ad – it must cause a **buyer to desire something** and inspire a willingness to act immediately. Yes, a person must immediately feel a strong wish to see your product and maybe to buy it. Otherwise, a prospect will be lost in the flow of online information. A call to action may include discounts, bonuses, gifts and a deadline indication such as "Apartments for newlyweds – a terrace for free! Up to December 1!"

Most social networks let an advertiser choose whether to **pay per click or per impression**. A cost, as well as for search engine advertising, can be limited by an advertiser who decides a maximum cost per click and a daily budget for advertising.

After clicking on an ad, a prospect is transferred to a link that takes them to an **external landing** or somewhere within a social network, for example, to a group. However, if your link leads to a group in a social network, you are likely to get just a member of the group. That's not bad, but we need a lead! Giving the main page of a corporate website as a link is, in most cases, not worthy as well, because usually there are tons of irrelevant information having nothing in common with the call to action. Using a landing (or, better, several landings) designed specifically for a campaign gives more flexibility and accuracy in testing.

The landing page **content** must be in accordance with the text of an advertisement. There is nothing worse than when a person clicks on a link and gets to a page where it is not evident how to get what was promised in an advertisement. Then, it turns out that the proposal is not valid anymore and it is just that the company has forgotten to correct an advertisement. A landing should contain a contact or an order form and provide all the arguments why people should fill it in now.

Initially, it makes sense to create **multiple ad variations**, which lead to **landing pages with variations**. Then you keep track of what works best. When doing lead generation in social networks you can imagine that **you are always in test mode**. This is because you need to constantly monitor the output in terms of sales and intermediate results of a campaign: impressions, clicks, leads conversions, and a cost per lead.

Yeah, maybe you will find a trick that will work for a long time, attracting qualified leads. But after some time, your target audience will be fed up with this technique, or the trick will be copied by competitors, so sooner or later you have to find new brilliant ideas.

Advertising in social networks, as well as in search engines, is managed online in real time. Be careful when **evaluating performance** and do not exaggerate the significance of clicks by themselves. The most important metric is **how many people, having clicked an ad, have become your customers, and what the final price per sale is.** For example, if a cost per click is $0.3 and the leads conversion is 4% (that is 1 of 25 visitors of the landing page fills in a contact form) and a sales conversion is 50% (each second lead makes a purchase) then the cost per lead is $0.3*100/4=\$7.5$, and the cost per sale is $7.5*100/50=\$15$. This price must be adequate in terms of the profit a company receives.

In conclusion, social networks also provide wide opportunities to promote a **company's image** by conducting corporate groups and communities. Employees like to keep track of corporate news through such channels. This is a great opportunity to show customers how a company's life bustles, how many people "like" it, and what a great team you have. In general, it is a demonstration of the fact that you are alive and well. Although it is not directly related to lead generation, it is a good occasion to remind your customers about your business, and gain more loyalty.

Social media advertising main steps

- Define the target audience.

- Choose social networks where your target audience spends time.
- Prepare ads (text, image).
- Create landings.
- Add conversion tracking tools.
- Test ads and landings.
- Campaign launch.
- Constantly check campaign results and analytics.
- Test and make improvements, if necessary.
- Identify leads, their qualification and scoring.
- Sales active phase.
- Transfer cold leads to the nurturing phase.
- Analyzing results, calculate conversion rate and ROI.

Ads on Individual Websites and Online Resources to Gain Leads

In addition to search engines and social networks, there are other places online where one can catch a lead – these are **thematic online resources,** such as online news, blogs, free services or educational websites of users with common interests. There are lots of such websites. In most cases, they give opportunities for **PR and brand advertising**. However, there is good potential for lead generation as well.

So, let us look at the whole process step by step. First of all, you create a list of specialized portals relevant to your topic. Aside from your own perspective and Google results, you can **study the online activity of your existing customers**, partners, competitors, journalists, and analysts or ask them about it. Then, you get in touch with managers of these websites. As a rule, they can provide statistics on the **number of visitors per month and their demographics**. This information can be checked with relative accuracy by a traffic metrics service like Alexa.com. Selecting suitable media, you agree about advertising options. The best thing is to do pay per click, not per impression, or just for time of placement of a banner. However, not all the resources will provide such terms.

Advertising format is individual and totally depends on the website. As a rule, the main types of promotion opportunities are as follows: banners of different sizes on a main page, pop-up windows, banners on secondary pages, text ads, and advertising articles. In general, the format is not so important for us. What matters most of all is that an advertisement should not just inform a person about your company, but also make him or her click on an ad and perform some action there. So a landing page should contain a **contact or order form with a reasonable call to action**. You have to give a visitor a compelling argument why it is necessary to fill in a form as soon as possible. As the campaign rolls on, you track the number of clicks on an ad, and the number of leads and sales.

In comparison to search engines and social network advertising, online mass media can be a very expensive method. On search engines and social networks, one can make ads with a minimum budget. But online portals are not interested in a minimum budget, at least when dealing with an advertiser directly (not through an advertising network like Google partners). Oh, it is not because they are greedy. In fact, it is just that their interaction with advertisers is not automated as well as on Google, so it is easier for them to deal with several large advertisers. However, without the automation of managing an ad, it will be hard to do tests and make adjustments. Therefore, it is better to use the advertisements proven by other more flexible channels.

Main Actions for Individual Websites' Lead Generation

- Define the target audience.
- Analyze online mass media in terms of their target audience, choosing a pool of relevant ones.
- Negotiate with websites' editors.
- Prepare ads (text, image).
- Develop landings.
- Add conversion tracking tools.
- Campaign launch and control of its realization.
- Identify leads, their qualification and scoring.
- Sales active phase.
- Transfer cold leads to the nurturing phase.
- Analyze results, calculate conversion and ROI.

And, last but not least, most of these individual websites partner with Google or other search engines. For example, Google **AdSense program** delivers Google AdWords ads to individuals' websites. Google then pays web publishers for ads displayed on their site, based on user clicks on ads or on ad impressions, depending on the type of ad. So by choosing this option, you may get an audience from different websites without a need to make many small contracts with them, which allows you to save time and finally money as you are able to deal with smaller budgets and to make as many tests as you like.

Print Mass Media and Outdoor Ads, Radio and TV for Lead Generation

Print media and outdoor advertising, as well as advertising on radio and television, in 95% of cases are used for **brand promotion**. This is necessary for producers of consumer goods such as food, cosmetics, household chemicals and electronics. Their sales are mostly done via retailers or online shops. Therefore, it is right to invest in the brand to boost sales. Just look at any advertisement of a perfume or a car model in a glossy magazine; often there are no contacts of specific stores where they can be bought. **Small businesses** and **companies working for narrow target groups** usually either do not need wide brand promotion or lack the funds for this.

To evaluate a return on each dollar spent on offline advertising, you can use the following lead generation know-how:

- Use advertising space with a **strictly defined target audience**.
- Focus not on the "wow effect" but on action; direct the person, using verbiage such as "**call**," "**write**," and "**fill out and send**." In addition, you should explain why this action must be performed right now.
- Estimate **how many calls are received as a result of an ad**. Besides indicating a separate number, it is possible to ask by phone from what source people have learned about your company. Also, you can print a special discount code or a bonus offer to track different ad results.
- Include **a contact form** for participation in some contest in a newspaper.
- Offer a person something for free by sending an SMS to a toll free number; it may be valuable information, a gift, a demo version, or an invitation to an event.
- Track the number of leads and the profit from them. By counting closed sales and money earned, you will be able to reach a conclusion whether or not to use this tool in future.

Testing offline advertisements may be pricey. Therefore, to reduce expenses for inefficient steps, it is better to check your ads and calls to action on your online advertising platforms. Then select the most effective variations and use them.

Main steps for "Offline" Advertising

- Define the target audience.
- Analyze the offline advertising space in terms of their target audience, choosing a pool of relevant ones.
- Choose resources and negotiations.
- Prepare an ad.
- Ad placement control.
- Identify leads, their qualification and scoring.
- Sales active phase.
- Transfer cold leads to the nurturing phase.
- Analyze results, calculate the conversion rate and ROI.

In conclusion, the main difficulty of offline advertising in terms of lead generation (besides its high price and breadth of audience) is an **inability to track the number of views** of your ad in **real time, and as a result – the number of leads and sales**. This resembles a shot in the dark. However, offline methods can perfectly support your other tactics to build brand awareness and may give some effect in terms of leads.

Marketing Pieces for Lead Generation
Armed by Testing

Having completed one version of marketing material, you're unlikely to get significant output the first time you use it. Even if a particular landing or e-mail gives you good results, you may be able to get more. Therefore, **be obsessive with regular testing**. It can save you a lot of money and time later. Tests that are not done for a check-in-the-box increase your conversion rate.

Let me tell you about several common traps regarding testing. First, do not panic over a little variation in results (like 5-10%); this does not necessarily mean anything. In fact, it may mean nothing, and happen due to circumstances. What you need to find out is a version that makes a difference in the results by at least 1.5 times. Second, **minor changes** such as editing body text, adjusting line spacing, repositioning buttons, playing with fonts and colors, and insignificant changes in a heading will hardly bring any notable difference in results. The important things that really influence a conversion rate are the **key message of a marketing piece and its call to action**. For landings, a picture plays a crucial role as well.

Main steps for successful testing

- Choose a target audience that you want to test.
- Make a concept or presupposition about what results you want to prove.
- Choose a testing method.
- Create marketing pieces with variables.

- Decide the amount of sample you'd like to test and the testing period.
- Measure results and reach a conclusion.
- Make edits.
- Repeat tests to prove or improve the marketing piece.

The most popular method of testing is A/B, or split testing. The concept is simple. A/B testing is done by comparing two or more versions of a marketing piece to see which one performs better. For example, you compare two web pages by showing two variants to similar visitors at the same time. As a result, you find out which one gives a better conversion rate.

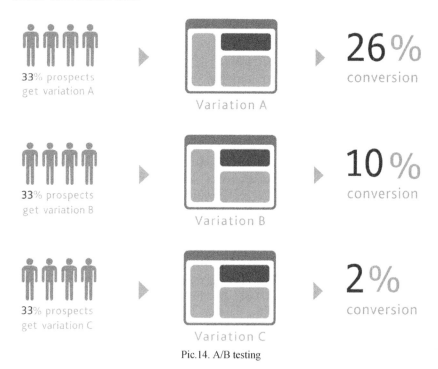

Pic.14. A/B testing

Multivariate testing is similar to A/B testing, but there are multiple variables. Its goal is to determine which combination of variations provides the best results. The difference with A/B testing is that A/B contains only one variable; in multivariate, we have as many variables as needed to discover an ideal combination. For example, if you have two elements in your material and two variants for each of them, you need to test four combinations. It saves time in comparison to A/B testing, which presumes you do everything by isolating one variable at a time.

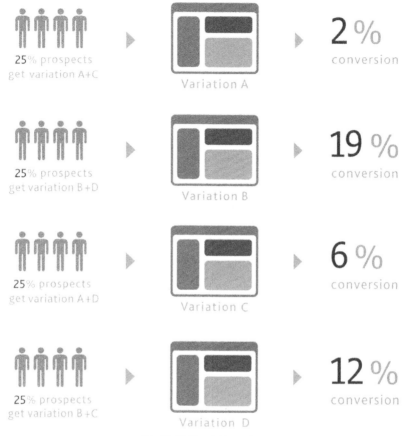

Pic.15. Multivariable testing

However, A/B and multivariable methods work best when an ad can be shown by an advertiser several times to a large target audience. Another testing approach is focused on conducting testing at the same time as receiving business results. This is called **multi-armed bandit testing**. In usual A/B or multivariable testing, you split a sample between equal groups and wait for the results. Scientifically, you are perfect. However, you may lose time and money by proving facts that are already evident from the very beginning. Using a multi-armed bandit method, one makes constant changes by allocating the most traffic or calls to the variant that has demonstrated the best results and continues to test other variants with whatever funds remain. This allows not only testing, which is not our goal by itself, but to get more leads sooner.

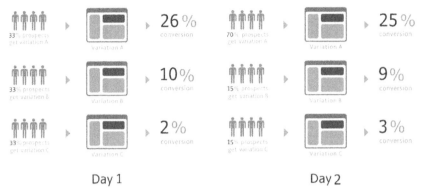

Pic.16. Multi-armed bandit testing

There are some arguments against **multi-armed bandit testing.** One of them is that the initially poorly performing version ends up receiving very little traffic and the statistical significance becomes based on small numbers. However, I think that this method is great when a sample of your prospects is small and you cannot run many A/B tests.

Generally, the **amount of prospects or leads** that is enough to consider a test finished depends on the size of your target audience. You can use the following approach:

- Landings are tested until we receive 100 leads and/or 1,000 unique visitors, for at least one week.

- E-mails are tested until we receive 100 leads and/or 1,000 openings.

- Call scripts are tested on a list of 500 prospects.

Actually, for small target groups one should be ready to **always work in test mode,** as the variations may be caused by multiple reasons not depending on your marketing piece; such reasons can be a change of competitive situation, a political and economic situation, an impact of other PR activities, etc. So be up for every move!

Landings for Boosting Sales

A **landing page** is a web page where visitors arrive after clicking on an online advertisement or a link. Basically, every page of any website can be called a landing. However, any page of a standard **corporate website offers many other functions aside from lead generation**; this page should be an all-inclusive informative resource about your company, not only for customers, but for potential employers, investors, the mass media, analysts, and partners. In this chapter, I shall speak about landing pages that are used purely for lead generation purposes and are designed specially to gain leads.

There is one more fact before we proceed. Let me highlight that these are **not landings that generate leads**. The key to success is an adjusted advertising campaign that consists **of pre-click marketing** – that is everything about search engines, e-mail marketing, online media, etc. – and **post-click marketing** – these are landings and their optimization. Pre-click marketing influences landing results to a large extent. A landing's goal is to deal with visitors after they click and encourage them to leave contact information.

The average landing page's **good conversion rate** is 3-5% (3-5 of 100 visitors become leads). However, there are companies that have a conversion rate higher than 12%. Is this what you want to reach? I suppose yes. But you should also remember that not only the quantity of leads plays a role but quality plays an important role as well; from this perspective, it is better to have fewer leads but more sales. Anyway, there is always a balance between the quantity of leads and their quality.

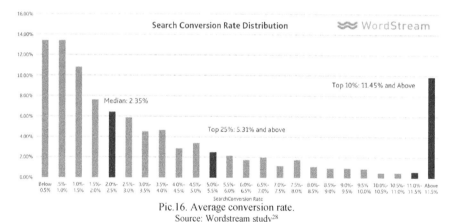

Pic.16. Average conversion rate.
Source: Wordstream study[28]

Key elements of a landing page

- Heading
- Brand and logo elements
- Pictures or video
- Description of your product

---

[28] Wordstream study, March 2014: http://www.wordstream.com/blog/ws/2014/03/17/what-is-a-good-conversion-rate

- Contact or order form
- Call to action
- Facts, figures, numbers, statistics
- References by customers
- Guarantees
- FAQ
- Contacts

The heading is one of the most important parts of a landing page. Most visitors read it and decide whether they stay or go. Remember: **one heading should be one idea.** Do not try to grab two or more birds in one fell swoop; for instance, do not offer to sell a product and test it for free. Your headline should be focused on a single idea. However, other options of what actions visitors can take may be offered by secondary buttons and minor calls to actions. The title must be unique. Otherwise, it makes sense to use different landings.

A heading should be as **simple as ABC**. Highbrow things fail. Wordplay, alliteration, and jargon only confuse a target audience and scare it. Headings written in short and simple language let a visitor grasp information quickly. Have you seen how simple the heading of MailChimp's landing is? **"Send better E-mail."** Previously, the title was simple as well, despite being a little longer, reading "Easy E-mail Newsletters," and it did not include a verb. Here we see how the heading was not only made shorter; furthermore, it focuses on the customers and their problems and offers a solution through the service. The heading does not advertise the service by itself without considering the customers' needs.

A **description of your proposal should follow**. The description should be detailed enough to make a purchase decision, but at the same time as short as possible in order to keep a buyer's attention. Perhaps your product is too complicated to be represented in few sentences. Excellent! Then, a landing should serve to establish contact with the target audience and allow them to get something valuable for free – information, consultation, industry benchmarks, etc. – rather than the sale of a product or service.

People believe numbers, especially those proven by independent statistics or analytics. Therefore, provide convincing facts. One can use a number of downloads, sales, customers, happy customer testimonials, returning customers or customers who referred your company to their friends and colleagues. It is important to be as exact as possible with your figures. In his book, *Tested Advertising Methods*,[29] John Caples describes a case: at the beginning of a campaign with an ad, there had been declared an indicator of 52.7% that was above the required standard for a product promoted. Sometime later, an advertiser decided to shorten this figure to 50% and then felt an outflow of customers. Customers had been leaving because the rounded figure of 50% did not sound as convincing as 52.7%.

Another convincing thing is feedback from other buyers. You may miss some technical feature or a detail of a product but you cannot miss how happy people are with your product. Provide **references and testimonials by other customers**; ideally, incorporate photos, real names, and titles.

Let us proceed to the next important part of a landing – a **contact or an order form**. Visitors should not leave the landing without sending their contact information. Once a person has an interest, the landing's goal is to make the most of it. Potential customers of products that have a long purchase cycle can be invited to download valuable material, register for an event, request a call, etc. To do this, people need to complete a short contact form. A general rule is to ask as few questions as possible. Another option is to ask only a name and e-mail on the first page and then on page 2 ask additional questions so that the potential customer does not feel interrogated or overwhelmed.

The next primary thing about landings is a **call to action.** A call to action is a proposal to do something. It should be clear, evident, and as short as possible. However, sometimes it is better to make it longer to preserve its obviousness; for example, use "download a free version" instead of just "download," which is unspecific (what? a white paper? a product itself or its demo?). I would say that a call to action is **the main thing concerning a landing**. So make it the hero of the story! Highlight it with contrasting colors and provide enough free space and visual prompts such as arrows, photos, or models. Thus, you may push a visitor to commit a target action.

A call to action should include a reason why one needs to fill in a contact form **right now. A delayed landing conversion is a lost conversion**. Your persistence must be well argued. Explain to customers why it is more profitable to send contact information today than tomorrow. You can appeal to a sense of fear ("There are only 10 last pieces!"), greed ("Save!", "2 for 1!"), love for freebies ("insurance as a gift!", "slippers for each pillow!") and other human weaknesses. However, the concept of urgency should be treated carefully. Sometimes, website visitors react negatively to these manipulations. How can you be sure that you are not overdoing it? Right you are – test it and you'll see.

---

[29] Tested Advertising Methods (Prentice Hall Business Classics), 1998 - John Caples, Fred E. Hahn

Another convincing thing you can do is a **guarantee** provided to ensure customers' satisfaction. There are lots of options. For example, an education center can guarantee that 67% of their students pass a certification exam. A food delivery company can guarantee that they deliver 98% of goods less than 15 minutes before a deadline or earlier or give 5% discount. Finally, there is a money back guarantee which applies to some businesses and helps create customers' certainty.

Another way to raise the conversion rate is by creating a section of frequently asked questions. Ideally, a landing page should include all the main objections of a potential client. Make sure that you can convincingly refute these objections. Is there a long installation? No, three minutes! Will a fertilizer be delivered to my hometown? Yes, anywhere in the country! Will a pizza be delivered before a deadline? We promise arrival on time and if late – delivery is FREE!

Brand and logo elements on a landing page should be well distinguished but should not distract visitors from their main goal: to do an intended action. A landing needs at least one **supporting image or short video.** A picture speaks louder than a thousand words, doesn't it? Not always. Dull pictures and clichés from content stock may kill a conversion. Visitors just ignore landings with standard pictures and do not try to understand the text. It is like banner blindness. A good video can raise the conversion rate if you are able to visualize how your service works; however, a poor video can slow the rate down. How to understand it? Oh, you know my answer – test, test, and test!

A landing should definitely include some **contact information for your company.** Being able to contact your company in different ways is a matter of visitor comfort. There are cases when one is unable to call (e.g., a woman sitting with an iPad near her baby sleeping or a person abroad on vacation), and there are people who prefer to speak rather than write letters or messages in online chat. However, sometimes the presence of a phone number or e-mail address on a landing hinders lead flow; it **distracts people from making an order NOW**, allowing them spending time on thinking and talking instead of filling in a contact form. So I suggest publishing a phone number somewhere at the bottom of a landing page. Those who need it will find it and others will not be distracted from submitting a form.

A notice about **navigation menus** illustrates how ambiguous everything can be, especially what concerns the "rules" of creating landings, and demonstrates that only testing gives an absolutely correct answer in each case. Most often, landing pages do not have a navigation menu. In most cases, it slows down conversion because it distracts visitors from a targeted action. But here is a **counterexample.**

SlideShop.com, an eCommerce website selling PowerPoint templates, used several versions of landing pages. The initial version of a landing contained a hidden navigation menu which appeared when hovering with a mouse. All pages had a promotional bar on the right that had a special offer, customer testimonials, etc. A version of the landing's design that has gained a maximum score as a result of A/B testing did not contain these extra banners and – what a surprise! – included a left navigation bar. This landing gave an **8.9% lift in user engagement and a 34% lift of people adding products to the cart**.[30] Here, a navigation menu added the feel of a comfortable environment for potential customers. To sum up, it is better to test your own landing than to follow patterns.

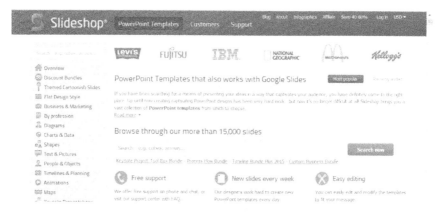

The following are the **main mistakes** to avoid in regard to landings:

- Do not transfer a visitor to a **corporate website's main page**. Make a landing. An exception is a company that has a very limited choice of goods (e.g., three variants of whitening stripes and nothing more).

- Do not have landing content that **does not correspond to the text of an advertisement**. Every second a visitor spends on a landing is extremely valuable. If desired information is not found quickly, visitors go away, and their next destination is possibly one of your competitors' websites.

- Do not have **one landing for different proposals**. A visitor does not know where to look next. Being confused, a visitor may postpone a decision until better days (which may never come).

- Do not have **external links**. It takes a prospect away from the main goal – filling in a contact form or initiating a call.

---

[30] Case study by VWO and Slideshop: Usability is not dead: how left navigation menu increased conversions by 34% for an eCommerce website
https://vwo.com/blog/usability-left-navigation-menu-bar-conversions-ecommerce-website/

- Do not have a **long landing**. Ideally, a landing should consist of 3-4 screens of scrolling.

- Do not **prompt non-immediate actions**. Most likely, if prospects are gone, they are gone forever. Landings are designed for immediate action.

- Do not neglect **testing**. Testing requires a constant monitoring of analytics that will help you build the most powerful landing.

There is a certain balance between the **seductiveness of an advertisement** getting a large number of clicks and the **landing working to get leads**. You can make a super-duper ad promising a dollar for 90 cents, but if at a landing people see that a commission is 20% of taxes, they will go away quickly. You will pay for clicks and lose money. Thus, if an ad is closer to your proposal, you will get fewer clicks but more leads. In general, quality and quantity are in perpetual confrontation and a perfect balance can be found only by testing.

Landings must be **easy to clone**. The first sample can be created by programmers and designers, but further edits should be easily done by marketing people. In the future, there will be millions of these edits, and having any extra element will slow the process down or just stop it. You can also use cloud software services for generating landings which are easy to create, and clone landings without any technical background.

There are lots of rules about landings and counter rules. People take them into account and try to make a creative landing that is distinct from competitors. Take into consideration the rule of a stereotype: users expect to see on your page something that fits their idea of what they should see. That is, if the top five of your competitors have a landing page of the same type, you do not need to reinvent the wheel and draft a new format. Just make **the best offer and the most powerful CTA**. By causing a cognitive dissonance in people's minds, you will not optimize lead conversion.

Call Scripts Bring Leads

A significant part of lead generation activities (sales by phone, arranging business meetings, events, market researches) includes making calls. Here a **call script** is the most important marketing material that influences success. Armed with a call script, managers will easily overcome a secretary and establish a positive contact with a decision maker. They will prioritize top issues concerning a product when presenting it to a decision maker to gain his or her interest.

In this section, I shall speak about call scripts that are **focused strictly on lead generation**. Closing sales by phone remains outside the focus of our interest. We have previously discussed that the process of finding customers and making sales are two different stages of work with a client. So the call script we look into now performs a single task – **finding leads and their qualification**.

It makes no sense to include in a lead generation script all the sales information about a product or a service. Moreover, it would be a failure if call scripts were so detailed that a lead generation manager could give a free consultation over the phone. A **prolonged conversation** is even dangerous for a conversion rate. It increases the probability that a potential customer will receive all the necessary information about a product before communicating with a sales manager, which offers fewer chances to influence one's purchase decision via sales people. As a result, a prospect either refuses or thinks for too long.

So **what is needed to prepare a good call script**? First of all, **understand the products or services sold**. No doubt you do. If a call script is done by an outsourcing company, it is necessary to provide **brochures, leaflets, analytics, press releases, and videos** to them. The most important information for an outsourcing agency to have concerns the target audience and the products' benefits for it. Additionally, you can add customers' references and case studies, as this is a nice talking point when dealing with a prospect.

The main thing about a lead generation call script is **its focus on the identification of an interest and the next step of a sales process**. For example, your sales cycle includes a business meeting. Then, the call script must provide some basic information about a product sufficient for suspects to understand whether it interests them; you should increasingly offer to discuss details during a meeting. It should sound like this: "If there is any interest – let us arrange a business meeting on Tuesday 10 a.m. or Wednesday any time." Prospects will be refocused from the fact that they need to make a purchase decision immediately to a question of whether they can spend an hour of time to learn more. A business meeting helps a decision maker to better evaluate whether a product is worthy and gives a sales manager the opportunity to start a sale to an interested customer, which transitions from a hard decision to an easy one!

A call script should contain several options for dialogue. Either your offer is of interest to a prospect or a person says "no" or has questions and objections. Or maybe he or she has all of that at the same time and in any order. A result of each conversation may be the following: an agreement to your offer, a delayed decision, a request for additional information, or a refusal (with a sufficient reason or not). This result is recorded in a CRM or other reporting system.

The **presentation of a call script** depends on your business' level of automation and your staff's qualifications for working over the phone. For call center operators, there is special software in which the following remarks are prompted depending on a respondent's reply. If a person feels sure he can speak without a pattern, it is enough to just have text with traceable logic.

Let's go to one of the most important things about call scripts. The **text of a call script should be written in a manner similar to a spoken language**, which is easy in pronunciation and moves from generalities to details. Use simple constructions. Advertising clichés, entangled verbal participle phrases, and structured lists are strictly forbidden. The text must be written so that it would seem that the one who pronounces it speaks like this daily when chatting with colleagues over a cup of coffee and a croissant.

~~~ *Tip* ~~~
*Smile while talking over the phone.
Yes, nobody sees it, but people can literally "hear" your smile on the other end.
The voice becomes softer and pleasant and the person
you are speaking with wants to hear more of it.
In addition, it perks up your mood as well.*
~~~

In the first round, a caller should introduce a **category of products** and services and him or herself. A caller needs to name an area in which you work and a category of problem solving. People sort and store information by category and if you don't provide a category for your product, your chances of getting it into your customer's mind are reduced significantly. This is so simple. It surprises me greatly why it happens so often that people calling cannot explain what they are speaking about. You may call it the elevator pitch of lead generation. You may try it hundreds of times before reaching an ideal.

Like any marketing piece, a call script should **focus on your customers' benefits**. It is well known that people are concerned about themselves. As marketing expert Orvel Ray Wilson perfectly noticed: "Customers buy for their reasons, not yours." Therefore, it is necessary to talk about them and tell them how their lives would be better if they buy your product. Sell the hole not the drill.

For lead generation in B2B sector, **numbers and references will be helpful**. Bring in statistics and successful projects carried out by your company. If you have a new business and there is nothing particularly spectacular to claim yet, you can talk about an experience of your team and draw attention to projects carried out by your employees as your team's success stories (not the corporate).

A call script should deal with **all possible objections and questions** that may arise. Some of them are **predictable.** They will concern your services or products and may include:
- What problem does it solve?
- What are its key functions?
- What are the advantages?
- How does it compare to X, Y, and Z?
- How much does it cost?
- What support/guarantees do you offer?
- How can I pay?

For corporate sales, one should be ready for questions about **compliance with any requirements** (certification, localization, compatibility with certain platforms, etc.), experience in a particular industry, and customer references.

Interestingly, the most difficult things to deal with are **simple questions and objections**. After all, in order to continue a conversation after "no money" or "no time," you need some experience and a passion for what you do. Here are some examples of simple questions and refusals that should not put you in a stupor:
- Why do I need this?
- And what?
- What's the point?
- How does it work?
- I don't understand anything.
- How does it differ from what I already have?
- I/we do not need it.
- I have no time.
- I have no money.
- It's expensive.
- Not this year.
- The management does not approve./The wife does not allow it.
- No. Just no.

These objections must be treated as questions. So, in response to "no time," you should try to clarify if there is no time at the very moment, or this week, month or year and suggest that you call back a person after this time has passed. In response to the words that a product is "expensive," one can reply: "A price should not hinder our possible cooperation," and explain the possibility to pay by credit, offer fewer product features, and propose making a purchase over the next month, year, or anything else that is affordable for their business. The main thing is to overcome an objection which may not be necessarily true, and proceed to the next level.

Below is a list **of questions for self-control during call script preparation**:

- Have all the advertising texts (complicated phrases and slogans) been reformulated into vernacular language? Does everything read as if spoken?

- Is the category of products/services evident from the first introduction? Is it clear what customer's problem the product or service solves?

- Can a person who knows nothing about your company immediately understand what it is about?

- Will new employees quickly become educated by this call script?

- Are the key advantages for a potential buyer included?

- Does the call script include answers to frequently asked questions and objections, including simple ones and more professionally phrased ones?

- Are there arguments convincing potential buyers to agree on a business meeting/download of a demo version/visit events, etc.?

- Is everything in the call script understandable (only widespread professional terms and jargon).

- Are all the definitions for lead generation managers provided and easily explained? It may happen that not every decision maker knows every term, so it is better to be careful.

A call script should include **lead qualification questions**. However, it is most likely that suspects will not give any information until they understand the reason for the call. Therefore, first of all, I recommend reaching an agreement on the next step of the sales cycle – a business meeting, a participation in a webinar, or taking part in a poll. After that, for example, to better prepare for a business meeting or for a commercial offer, you may ask additional information to characterize a prospect as a cold, warm or a hot lead. If at this stage you suddenly get a completely unsatisfactory answer that disqualifies a lead, it is possible to vocalize with regret that, unfortunately, your services are unlikely to suit a respondent, as they better suit another target audience. Of course, I assume that such cases will be very few if you have selected your target audience properly. In any case, practice shows that this approach provides better results than trying to qualify a lead before clarifying its willingness to make the next purchase cycle step.

Lead Generation Letters

A well-done lead generation letter can be sent to hundreds and thousands of people but is should look **as if it is written to a single person**. The main thing is to create the feeling of a personal approach. This provides the maximum number of responses. This rule is fair for both genres – e-mail messages and letters sent by offline mail. A personal letter in lead generation has the following features:

- It is sent to a certain person.
- It describes a proposal that is directly related to the interests of an addressee.
- It contains a name or a surname (maybe with an honorific, depending on the traditions of the industry).
- It is written in a simple and polite style.
- It does not have advertising stamps.
- It is sent to one person once.
- It provides a brief presentation of you and your business.
- It has a signature with all your official contacts.
- It contains a notification after a signature about the policy of sending of this e-mail.
- It creates a sense of individual approach.

First, let us consider **e-mail**. The subject should be slightly intriguing so that an addressee wants to open it, and, of course, it should reflect the essence of the letter's body. Do not write anything like "a unique offer" or "cheap shipping" or anything like what you ever see in your spam box. According to my experience, the following kinds of subjects have one of the best open rates: "a meeting on June 5 on BI" (an addressee immediately thinks: "What meeting? Did I forget something?") or "a question about vacations" (a first thought: "What's wrong with vacations? Haven't we agreed on everything?!") or "Ksenia, you have forgotten a dress in your cart" ("Oh, how sweet, you take care of me!"). Do not send e-mails without a subject; some e-mail services treat this as a spam.

~~~ *Tips for Subject Lines From MailChimp*[31] ~~~

- **Include Localization.** *Personalize a message with a recipient's first or last name or even a city to improve open rates.*
- **Use Different Subject Lines.** *Newsletters tend to start with high open rates but these rates decrease over time. Keep your content fresh and don't repeat the same subject line for each campaign.*

---

[31] Source: http://kb.mailchimp.com/campaigns/previews-and-tests/best-practices-for-email-subject-lines

- ***Keep Subject Lines Short*** – *50 characters or fewer. Most people quickly scan subject lines to decide if they'll open or ignore the e-mail.*
- ***Use Promotional E-mails Effectively.*** *Promote contests and give-aways in your campaigns to reconnect with inactive subscribers. Send subscribers a poll or survey to find out what type of content they're interested in. Offer a free gift or service as an incentive to complete the poll or survey.*

~~~

Ideally, the **text of an e-mail should take up one screen** without needing to scroll the mouse. If you still have something else to say, put this information after a signature, attach a file, or provide links. The key secret about e-mails is simple: **the shorter the e-mail, the more effective it is**. However, absolute brevity is appropriate only for e-mails to people with whom you have interacted before; otherwise, it seems rude.

The **main idea** of a message should be clear from the first paragraph. To reinforce an effect, it should be repeated at the end. For example, if the goal is to agree on a business meeting, do not beat around the bush. Offer a date and time in the very beginning. If some plans change, it is easier to rearrange for a new time than to agree on it from zero. And in order to avoid conflicts, send out such letters in small batches, changing the time proposed. A sample of a beginning of a letter:

"Dear Steve,

We met at the CeBIT exhibition and I would like to speak with you regarding your database security in detail.

Can we arrange a call at 3 or 4 pm London time on Tuesday?

Let me remind you that..."

Or: "Hello Margaret,

My name is Jane Anderson and I would like to contact you regarding your sales team result improvement.

We provide sales training and I will be happy to tell you how other car dealers have achieved a 15-20% growth in their sales after our training course.

I propose to arrange a call on Thursday afternoon, for example, at 11 a.m...."

It's time for another lead generation secret. A very effective tool for e-mailing is to send a **reminder a few days after a first letter**. Of course, it should be addressed only to those recipients who have not responded earlier. In contrast to the first letter, which may contain a rather detailed proposal, a reminder should consist of three or four sentences. Its main idea is the following: "Could you please confirm you received my letter? Can we... / Could you...?" Since this e-mail looks even more personal and requires a short answer, you will get a large response rate that at least will save time for further calls and ideally will provide a number of leads.

A **snail mail letter** strictly follows epistolary etiquette. Today, it is sent to people whom you do not know and/or are unable to contact via other means of communication. An offline letter presumes you can write **more**. In contrast to e-mail, brevity here is not the soul of wit. A person can read even a very long text (one or two pages) if at first glance, he or she becomes interested. So try to assure, please, and prove.

Offline letters should **trigger some action of their recipient**. Try to simplify an understanding of what you want your addressee to do and why it makes sense; e.g., to call to make an order by November 15. Highlight it at the beginning and at the end of a letter. From your message it must be clear why it is necessary to make an order as soon as possible. One example is offering a special bonus, a discount, or a gift. To ensure the simplicity of reacting to an offline letter, sometimes marketers insert an envelope with a return address and a template application. It works even today in our digital world; for example, receiving a discount plastic card for a retailer for a target audience that are not frequent users of computer devices.

The style and format of snail mail is generally more formal than for e-mails. Today, it does not always require all the official attributes of an ideal classical business letter such as a corporate template with a logo, formal salutation, official style, etc. It all depends on the product you are promoting. If you work for a bank or an insurance company, these attributes are definitely required. If you have a hotel or restaurant, they will only increase distance, and this is not what you need. It is definitely a must to be courteous to your addressee within the proposal, in any case.

At the end of a letter, both e-mail and offline, there must be a **signature with contact information**. In fact, a signature is enough for experienced people to understand what you want from them. It should be easy to contact you. If possible, provide a cell phone number. In offline letters, you can add a handwritten signature, even if it is just printed. It is better to list your e-mail with your signature in case the body of the letter will be copy-pasted and sent to another person, which could lead to someone losing your contact information (another reason for that is that in some e-mailing software a sender's e-mail may be "lost" and replaced with a name when an e-mail is forwarded). In addition, you **must** give addressees an opportunity to remove themselves from your mailing list or unsubscribe.

~~~ *Tip* ~~~
A Sample of a Footer (follows the signature)
Please consider the environment before printing this e-mail.
This message may contain confidential or legally privileged information and is intended solely to the mentioned addressee. If you receive this message by mistake, please immediately notify the sender by e-mail and please immediately delete the message. You must not copy this message, use it for any purpose, or disclose its content or a part thereof to a third party. The provisions and/or statements contained in the present message shall not be considered as an offer, official statement, or obligation to the intended addressee indicated in the message. But, if

you would like to stop receiving any further messages, click here or write me back and I will not e-mail you further.

~~~

And last but not least: thank people for reading your letter but do not be overly gratuitous. Demonstrate your appreciation for them finding time to answer, even if they refuse (you may save time for further telephone calls). Recipients should feel their unique replies are important to you. **Sound like a human but do not overdo emotion.** Do not write in an impartial and formal style; use a conversational tone and style to show that the response was specially written to the addressee. It is even possible to use emoticons or make a text a bit lumpy to raise a level of personalization.

Marketing Lists as a Foundation for Direct Sales

Marketers say: "Give us a good contact list and we will move the whole world."[32] Marketing lists of contacts **are the main asset of lead generation managers** who assist direct sales. Having a good marketing list saves time which is, unlike other resources, indispensable. They allow lead generation managers to focus on communications and lead qualification.

An inescapable feature of any marketing contact list is that it eventually **"runs out."** First, it runs out because you step by step acquire all the leads and refusals and no new possibilities remain. Second, any static list of contacts is outdated by approximately 30% per year. Some specialists change jobs, companies merge, acquisitions are made, and offices move from one venue to another. In general, life thrums along and a contact list must be constantly updated to track these changes. That is why it is important to use every possibility to update and enlarge contacts. After all, new contacts mean new leads, and new leads are new sales!

Companies use the following methods of enlarging their contact lists:
- social networks;
- online mass media;
- business directories like Yellow Pages;
- professional business alliances and associations;
- marketing list providers;

---

[32] "Give me a place to stand and with a lever I will move the whole world." - an original quote by Archimedes (c. 287 BC – c. 212 BC), a Greek mathematician and philosopher.

- hosted and third-party events;
- cold calling;
- companies' industry ratings;
- partner resources;
- official statistics and legal information;
- personal contacts of employers;
- geo-marketing around a territory.

The procedure of **making marketing lists** (not buying) is the following: first of all, a manager compiles a list of a company's target audience from online business directories, websites of professional associations, and companies' directories. Try to think out of the box to save time when making such a list. For example, to find companies with a good marketing budget, a manager may take a look at sponsors of professional events, compile their list, and start working with it. After having made a list of companies, it is necessary to find a particular decision maker. It is possible to do this using social networks, search engines, mass media, corporate website, and making cold calls.

This is a rather time-consuming (and, consequently, expensive) process. An alternative option is to **buy contacts from marketing list providers**. Some companies sell business data while others provide consumer e-mails. Marketing list providers differ by their **source of information**. For example, a source can be a special data crawler that gets all available information on the Net. Another provider may use crowdsourcing when users add and update contacts and get contacts for free or buy them. It is like a commercialized Wikipedia of business contacts. Another contact list provider gathers information by compiling all event participants. With lists for purchase, be careful about the legislation of the country where you do lead generation. For example, in Russia, private persons' contact information is not allowed for sale or resale; you may legally obtain this data only if a person provides you their contact information and has given you consent so that you may be allowed to store and use these data for a purpose for which they have been given to you.

~~~ *Tip* ~~~

Sometimes, organizers of events for a narrow target group publish a list of registered participants on a website or provide information about last year's participants to persuade you to take part this year. What a great opportunity to get names of new prospects without paying a penny!

~~~

It is also possible to hire a **lead generation agency** that has industry experience to build a list of prospects. However, I think that if starting collaboration with a lead generation agency, it makes sense to order a full leads gaining campaign. Anyway, tasks differ and sometimes even a contact list compilation and actualization should be done by high-level communication managers specializing in your industry.

Software to Optimize Lead Generation Processes
Innovations to Serve Marketing

Lead generation is a part of marketing that requires a **scrupulous execution of business processes**. Any act of carelessness may result in reputation risks, loss of trust, or other issues which will incur additional cost in the time spent correcting them.

One step which can be taken to lessen the impact of human error and keep mistakes at a minimum is **automating the process of lead generation**. Let's talk about software that can help lead generation managers work more effectively, which will bring in more qualitative leads with less effort overall.

Customer Relationship Management (CRM) System

A Customer Relationship Management system is a **space for compiling data about lead generation, marketing, sales, and customer support**. This computer system stores contact information of customers and keeps track of any communications with them such as customer requests, letters, results of negotiations, commercial offers, etc. In the most primitive way, CRM is similar to an address book and an organizer that keeps a history of your interactions with clients.

CRM enables **sales and marketing people to work together**. It allows updated contact information to stay in a single space; it also manages team tasks regarding contacts and opportunities and tracks contacts' status. To put it simply, a member of a team or a head of department does not need to run around an office from one desk to another trying to clarify information, create reminders, or collect results. Everything is available on a laptop or a mobile screen.

© Lead Generation: Theory and Practice by Ksenia Andreeva

I would like to make it clear that CRM **does not work wonders by itself.** CRM is only a tool for employees to keep prospects, leads, and sales data, to report on completed actions and set goals for the future. It must be a mandatory reporting system for everyone engaged in sales and direct marketing. There are many companies that may have implemented CRM, but are not updating the pertinent info daily and thus aren't using it to its full capacity. As a result, these companies say that CRM "does not work". Of course!

For a small number of contacts CRM is not only less effective, but may even do harm; it will take time and money, yet still may not yield the desired results. If a company has 20-30 prospects, a good old magnet billboard as a sales pipeline may be enough. It can be updated on a daily basis, moving magnets with customers' names from one column to another; for instance, the magnet moves from "Prospect" to "Meeting", "Business Proposal", "Negotiations" and finally "Sale".

CRM provides **wide analytical opportunities**. You can analyze employer performance, evaluate results of marketing campaigns, and forecast the sales' pipeline. You can monitor the conversion rate of prospects into leads and the rate of leads into sales. First of all, to estimate the ROI of a marketing activity, it is necessary to specify in CRM the source of a contact list. Then, you start to work on it, adding and attaining leads and other results. After a while, some leads will become sales. You are able to assess the overall effect and make conclusions about whether to continue using this or that marketing activity. As a result, you increase the efficiency of your marketing budget's utilization.

It is also important that a CRM system **decreases the dependency upon human factors**. While there is no doubt that a team is the core tenet for every business, no one is secure from a situation where their best sales or lead generation manager retires. Without a CRM system, it becomes hard to share information about potential customers with those colleagues who go on working with them. Most likely, it will turn into an endless and senseless rigmarole. Typically, sales managers usually take with them their contacts and a certain amount of information related to them; this is a very dangerous situation. Using a CRM system will reduce the negative consequences of an employee's dismissal. Of course, if CRM is used properly and all contacts are stored in the system, the transfer of details from one manager to another is fairly simple.

The question of which CRM to choose depends primarily on its **concept, price, functionality, and alignment with your business goals**. Your current information landscape plays an important role. Perhaps you already have a certain set of IT solutions, and it makes no sense to engineer an ecosystem of solutions hodgepodged from different providers. In this scenario, CRM can play a role in reducing your overall workload and by association, operating costs.

E-mail Marketing Software

E-mail marketing software can save a lot of time in **sending letters and processing results**. Most e-mail marketing services have the **following features** aside from actual mailing: choosing a preset time for mailing, e-mail personalization (insertion of a name or any other element), and design tools. They automate the process of unsubscribing and cleaning up invalid subscriber info. In addition, they provide analytics on mailing results, including the number of e-mails delivered, opened, forwarded, and unread. It may be also possible to see a comparison of your results to statistics standard throughout your industry, such as an average open and unsubscribe rate.

Another great thing about e-mail software is the workflow of e-mails that may be **scheduled or triggered by a user's behavior, preferences, and previous sales**. It is an advanced feature that may be available for premium accounts. Lead nurturing by e-mail is usually powered by such a workflow as **it is necessary to send leads the same e-mails at different times** (and consequently different emails at the same time). For example, whenever people subscribe to your newsletter, a welcome e-mail is sent, followed by a coupon for a discount, then a case study or article, and finally a link to a webinar or proposal to arrange a call. Or, a person adds a product to their cart and leaves your website without making a purchase; this is a great opportunity to send along a reminder the next day! **After a purchase,** you may send a thank you letter, a link to additional products that may complement a purchase, and – after the goods are shipped – a request for feedback. Unlike conventional newsletters that are related to important company events, here you can automate an individual approach to every lead depending on parameters you specify.

E-mail software also provides options for running **A/B testing,** which allows you to check which message version works best of all in terms of the open, click, and unsubscribe rate. Another great benefit for online vendors is the ability to track sales and calculate ROI. It is essential to take into account that some e-mail software can be integrated with CRM systems with the added bonus of faster synchronization of contacts in both systems.

However, as with CRM, it makes no sense to reinvent the wheel. **MS Office tools** can also be used to merge a Word document with an Excel spreadsheet, and send via e-mail using Outlook. One can even add personalization features such as an addressee or company name. However, aside from the overload of manual work after each mailing, one should take into account that Internet and SMTP (a protocol for e-mail delivery) providers have an **anti-spam policy**; because of this, what seems like an eager initiative to increase your company's outreach will seem suspicious on their end. Some of them can block your sending account if you send more than 10 letters per minute.

E-mail software suites generally provide a **robust set of options for spam control and administration** which include various algorithms that calculate the number of bounces, the number of unsubscriptions, reports, letter content, e-mail list, and credibility of a sender. Your slick operation can be blocked posthaste if your subscribers have forgotten that they opted-in to receive your e-mails from you. Oh yes, I understand – the life of a lead generation manager is hard!

To sum it up, utilizing the power of e-mail in marketing is easy provided you have software for that, and does not require a long and pricey installation. E-mail systems save time on processing results, which in turn allows you to focus on leads.

Landing Page Generators

Landing page generators offer an easy tool to create landings just in few minutes, offering a variety of templates that **can be edited without any technical background or computing expertise**. Any person who knows how to use basic Office tools should be able to learn how to perform their own edits in a very short time. One may change a template any way they like to personalize it; however, when making formatting changes, keep in mind that if you make too many of them the end result may not appear as attractive or professional as the initial, unedited version. If none of basic templates suit you and you'd prefer something more unique, you can typically use your own designs in conjunction with other functionality of landing page generators.

As for the other functionality: what I like most of all are the **powerful tools for tracking leads**. With a landing page generator, you may see the number of leads generated by each of your landings and store them in one place, or have leads automatically recorded in your CRM and/or integrated e-mail software. If you do not have CRM, just have a look at the relevant functionality of landing page generators; there are many businesses for which its basic features will be enough for managing leads and turning them into opportunities and sales.

You can **easily clone and edit your landing page template**, which is a useful tool for running tests and analytics. There are additional valuable features such as tracking clicks and conversions. The analytics you obtain will be visualized, which will provide insight into estimating the best workable landings in terms of visitors to leads, leads to sales conversion, and secondary data such as bounces, unique visitors, and different conversions.

Landing page generators are usually **affordable for every budget**, which gives them one more plus in my eyes. Creating similar features on your own makes sense only if it is the core of your business and you are not limited by your budget and time. Otherwise the architecture, development, and testing of such applications will take considerably longer; since time is money, this will result in elevated costs.

Knowledge Management

Each company needs to **establish a common knowledge base** viewable online through a corporate portal. By accessing it, employees can independently obtain the necessary information at a sufficient level. For lead generation and marketing specialists, this is especially important because they have to maintain and update information quickly enough to remain relevant. Through this base, they are able to use information about other projects and expand their competence. They do not have to distract colleagues with basic questions or remind them about updates. In addition, for companies having several distributed offices in different countries or cities, it is often the only opportunity to share experience with faculty working in other venues.

The most important information for lead generation to be stored in a knowledge base usually includes:
- a lead generation manual;
- call scripts;
- texts of letter templates;
- brochures for products or services;
- case studies;
- interviews and publications;
- expert opinions on the subject;
- videos and podcasts;
- necessary contacts.

It is important to instill in staff that **adding and updating the corporate library is everyone's responsibility**, which increases the efficiency of the team overall. Then they will make changes, add and update information, or request colleagues to update their side of things on the portal. Eventually, they will accept and embrace it on realizing their ability to get up-to-date information anywhere in real-time.

The methods of organizing corporate knowledge vary on the required functionality and budget. Corporate portals can be preconfigured or customized especially for your company. Some CRM systems also include features for uploading documents, grouping them, and searching for content. These solutions make it possible to manage the company's institutional knowledge and provide users access control. This is invaluable for large corporations that cannot manage each employee's authority, and combine them into groups.

There is no doubt that a corporate knowledge portal is **useful not only for large enterprises, but for the small ones as well**. The time of small business managers is especially valuable. The free online storage service Google Drive (previously known as Google Docs) can be used to store information, upload documents, and share them with other users.

Collaboration and To-Do Lists

Traditional functions of a lead generation manager are as follows. Someone should be contacted by phone; someone needs a letter; someone should be congratulated on Construction Workers' Day, etc. These tasks are best managed by a CRM or call center system that is designed to organize work over contacts and calls. However, lead generation managers can also perform tasks that are not directly related to a particular contact. Such tasks may include the preparation of call scripts, letter templates, and generating or purchasing contact lists. Some of these may have stages that need to be signed off on by several authorities from various departments.

Project and task management may be a module of a CRM system or corporate portal or may be integrated with them. Surely, it is more efficient to try to use solutions provided by one vendor than to switch back and forth from different unintegrated interfaces. Using other vendors' solutions may be tempting – they may have a free version and the cost savings are alluring – however, long-term experience shows that having different interfaces, even if some or even all of them are free, will fail since staff will not have the time to work in a variety of software.

A project and task management system supports **collaborative teamwork while setting a plan for tasks, monitoring achievements, and allocating responsibilities**. It notifies a person about a new task prioritized or delegated and indicates a change of status in tasks assigned to colleagues. In short, no one has a chance to forget something. Additional settings allow an implementation of algorithms for a flow of related tasks. Typically, most of these solutions have mobile access. This enables constant awareness about a project's state of affairs wherever you are, be it in a business meeting, at a lunch, on a business trip, etc.

I believe the task management tool is an option which every business vying for process improvement should possess. Without it, a manager may sooner or later become overwhelmed due to the **sheer volume of information to retain and control**. There are some managers that enjoy keeping on top of everything but personally I do not think this is a wise approach for a business owner. There was a curious business case where the top management of one large airline company had forcibly sent all of their top managers **on vacation for a month and then evaluated how their departments worked** without them. Those departments which functioned as well without a boss as with him or her were rewarded a bonus; those that ceased to work or became inefficient were fired. The moral of this story is that human dependency allows for a disorganization of critical processes. If you want to go on vacations (at least sometimes!), try to avoid it, and especially try to avoid it if you are a business owner and want to eliminate risks.

Marketing Lists Services

I have already spoken about services that provide **marketing contact lists.** Some of them are even integrated with CRM systems. They allow you to save time on web-surfing, since having a contact list including a name, a title, a company industry, an e-mail, and a phone number makes cold calls and their preparation more effective. Direct contacts are the most precious information lead generation managers of B2B companies can obtain. This information helps to get through a secretary and reach a decision maker. Integration with CRM systems enables you to import contacts directly into CRM.

When using such services, a marketer **searches by relevant criteria:** these searches can be by location, a vertical, the size of a business, turnover, title, department, company, or person's name. From this criteria, contacts lists can be purchased. Most services give a guarantee that contacts are up-to-date and offer a return policy for defunct or out-of-date contacts. This differs from service to service, but there is usually some time to check if the contacts are "alive," and to exchange them for others.

Marketing Automation Software

The problem a company faces when starting to choose different types of software is their integration. Most large e-mail services, landing page generators, and CRM systems offer integration. However, **integration is always a question of additional effort**.

All-in-one marketing automation software services suggest **a single space** for managing all such marketing tools such as e-mail marketing, pay per click ads, landings, websites, social networks, content creation, and analytics. But this is more than just a single space: the **lead management features of such systems include lead scoring, lead nurturing, and prospecting.** Such systems can determine visitors' companies by IP and evaluate their actions in this respect.

These are **versatile systems with a large functionality**, and they are typically quite expensive. Usually, they suit the goals of **large and medium enterprises**. The implementation period can also be quite prolonged, but after implementation, all the work in the system is done by the marketing managers themselves without the assistance of IT. The main challenge of working in such a system becomes the creation of loads of content – the system will take care of all other lead management actions and analytics.

Call Center and IP Telephony

IP telephony is an effective way to reduce the cost of international and long-distance telephone services, with the added benefit of being able to track outgoing calls done by each manager, save their records, and retrieve stats based on the number of calls, their geography, and duration.

The **number of calls influences the number of leads** – this is simply statistics. If you make zero calls, you will have zero leads and consequently, zero sales. Otherwise, it will be like in this funny tale: A man who was in financial difficulty started to pray. "Listen God," he said. "I know I haven't been perfect but I really need to win the lottery. I really need this money. My mom needs surgery and I have bills to pay. Please let me win the lottery." He repeated this ritual every day, groaning and crying. Finally, the clouds opened up and a booming voice was heard from above – "John, when will you at least *buy* a lottery ticket?'"

Maximizing call quality can be achieved through the configuration of advanced settings in your call center software. Such settings allow you to manage several operators and automate their work even if they are based in different offices, or at home. Predictive dialing features save time on dialing phone numbers and actually getting through to someone.

Here, the most overwhelming aspect is the analysis of call information. This allows management to observe:

- the number of calls made per telemarketer;
- the conversion rate of cold calls to leads (so the best telemarketers can be identified quickly);
- the average time of conversation (this helps to understand what resources are necessary for each project);
- the number of calls required to convert a prospect into a lead (valuable for determining your cadence!).

Many call center software providers offer basic CRM functionality, and it is a good option to have a look at it before assessing the need to integrate it with a classic CRM. For some businesses, CRM is not a prerequisite; however, practically every business today needs e-mail software, which should somehow be integrated with your general contact database.

Call center software is **ideal for the management and analyzing of a high volume of calls**. However, its basic functionality typically does not denote high-level personalized work with customers, which may result in your telemarketers coming off as too impersonal, or generic. This should be taken into account when estimating which call center software features will prove valuable to your team.

Shared Calendar Apps

When scheduling business meetings, a lead generation specialist needs to **manage the timetable of sales managers**. Let me remind you that a business meeting is a must-have step for many products. A meeting with decision makers is a chance to persuade them to make a purchase or close a deal. In this regard, a lead generation manager immediately offers a meeting time as soon as someone reveals interest. It is necessary to migrate the decision maker from a difficult question ("Do I need this service for a million dollars right now?") to a simple one ("Can I spend an hour of Thursday morning to find out how my business can benefit from this service?").

So, it would be easier if your sales managers' daily timetable is **transparent to the lead generation employees in order to streamline process for allocating time for meetings and conference calls**. This will help reduce the back and forth of approving the date and time of a meeting, avoid "shaking-up" one's schedule, and keep further coordination at a minimum. Of course, sometimes a very important sale appears suddenly and plans need to be changed, which will cause a meeting to be rescheduled. In any case, you will save a lot of time for lead generation and sales managers, since instead of wasting precious hours on logistics, they will focus on searching for new leads and handling prospective customers who have already been discovered.

As well as a task management system, calendars can be part of a **CRM system or a corporate portal's functionality**. At NWComm, we sometimes work on customers' applications for calendars when we do lead generation for them. This allows us to minimize both the customer's and our own efforts devoted to confirming time periods available for meetings. As part of setup, some tools will create reminders for the meeting time and location and send a notification to all participants.

PART 3. A LEAD GENERATION TEAM

Building a Team
The Myth about "Easy" Marketing and the Reality

Recently, the notion has been gaining traction that gaining leads is a low-skilled activity. Some companies have thought that it is enough to hire a freelancer for pay per click advertising or have students making cold calls through the Yellow Pages to secure new customers. Alas! First, these people lack the most important thing – an understanding of your prospective buyer. Second, this temporary staff will likely not stay with you for an extended period of time. If, after a couple of months, they move onto different employment opportunities, all the effort and resources invested in educating them and involving them in your business will be for naught. This results in lost time, and as we all know, lost time is lost money. While you will gain experience, it takes proper knowledge to understand the sales process and cultivate leads; however, the limited experience gained will not help your lead generation campaign.

Marketing efforts aimed at lead generation are the most important part of direct sales companies' promotional strategy. These efforts may be the most difficult part of a campaign, but also have the most impact on profit. As such, it is desirable to use personnel who are professionals.

For **managers whose responsibility it is to seek new and prospective customers**, it is necessary to:
- be aware of the marketing and sales tactics of a company;
- know the basic concepts surrounding lead generation;

- understand the goals and objectives of lead generation activities for a company;
- be able to effectively communicate by phone and e-mail, to speak, listen, and report;
- find common ground with the sales department and understand its priorities;
- possess the relevant computer skills or learn information technologies that make lead generation work more efficient;
- have a strong desire to work in (and understand the importance of) lead generation for your business.

In this chapter, I shall discuss different specialists involved in the lead generation process. **These are lead generation telemarketers, copywriters, and contact list managers**. Of course, some of these roles can be performed by a single manager. However, it is important to understand the specific functions behind each activity and be able to switch gears; for example, by 2 in the afternoon, I am a copywriter – after that, I must act as a telemarketer.

Telemarketers

Lead generation telemarketers need to understand the **details and specific problems facing their target audience**. They need to know the main **features of promoted products and services**, and typically, a general product knowledge can be obtained rather quickly. Of course, a telemarketer must also use proper grammar and possess a voice that is pleasant to listen to. They need to understand the **lowdown of making cold calls to get to a decision maker** in their target audience, and how to **talk to people professionally.** All these things are important. But they are not enough!

Lead generation telemarketers require a psychological understanding of interlocutors; their goals and objectives, their hopes and fears. In addition (pay attention!), they **must be able to sympathize with people**, not as a whole, but with each person they encounter. Since I have discovered this, I hire only people that have a positive attitude and who can maintain that attitude with the world and the people they speak with. It is very important! After all, people who make many calls hear so many negative things starting from rude refusals and ending with lamentations on one's personal and professional problems. This brings us to another requirement for a lead generation telemarketer – a **stable mind**. Lead generation by phone is not an emotional business. Timid boys and girls will not do well; we need seasoned people.

The secret that helps me to "love" a person on the other end of the phone is that I **really want help him or her** and try my best to understand his or her position. I try to imagine one's concerns and worries: a budget here, a deadline there, correcting their predecessor's mistakes here, and let's not forget that boss who always rushes! It is amazing that some people – even before saying anything relevant to a topic – just need to be heard. Perhaps it is not a confession, but merely a deep sigh. You have to hear this sigh to fully communicate. However, a lead generation telemarketer should distinguish a conversation that may end with an identified interest from a chat that exemplifies a free crisis center.

The main thing is to love your prospects

© Lead Generation: Theory and Practice by Ksenia Andreeva

The next important characteristic of a lead generation warrior is **mastery of cultural constructs and paradigms**, which are necessary to keep up a conversation with a potential client. It is possible (and even very possible) that your prospective customers are well-educated people with years of professional and private experience and great intuition. A key factor of cold call success is that the prospect should not be able to guess that he is #674 from a contact list and that the call is made by a call script. An ideal situation is when a lead generation telemarketer sounds like a business development or marketing manager, or like a personal assistant to a top-manager for whom the meeting is being arranged.

To break the ice of the first cold call, a lead generation telemarketer may choose not to follow a strict pattern, while still remaining within the bounds of ethical behavior. Sometimes a **sense of humor** helps. Once, we had a lead generation project for a telecommunication equipment vendor. We had to call resellers who had previously bought something but did not have an official VAR/VAD contract. The purpose of these calls was to sign a formal partnership agreement and to remind the resellers about the vendor and its products. Signing an official partnership agreement would add the reseller to a partner program, which has many benefits for raising one's loyalty like discounts and bonuses, presales support, joint marketing activities, etc. So we made calls. The CEO of one reseller first refused to sign a partnership contract as he had no interest in its benefits. He explained that previously he had been purchasing vendor's production without an agreement, and that he knew the price list and relevant contacts, where to buy, how to ship, and so on. In response, the telemarketer (a very polite young woman) said: "It's great that we've already been working together! Let's finally make our relationship official!" The man laughed, thought for a moment, and went forth with signing the agreement. Of course, this does not meant that the reseller immediately bought tons of telecom equipment; nevertheless, a positive contact was established, and cooperation expanded. Achieving small results incrementally may garner additional purchases, and ultimately increase your company's profit.

Copywriters and Writers

The preparation of lead generation and nurturing letters, call scripts, landing pages, website texts, and other **marketing pieces** that can quantitatively deliver leads is a matter of other qualification. However, **the best lead generation copywriters I know have experience in both sales and marketing generation**.

Effective lead generation copywriters know what a conversion rate is, the average response and open rate, and the cost per lead – everything we have discussed before. They understand that their goal is to create texts that gain the maximum number of leads which will result in sales. As a rule, they actively test their texts, and gain the experience of creating marketing pieces that achieve a maximum conversion rate step-by-step.

It is important for a variety of lead generation texts to be in accordance with their genre. For example, a call script requires the use of spoken language that is focused on "capturing" buyers; such language initiates a dialogue, then qualifies, and finally actuates steps towards decision making that will result in a purchase: such as agreeing to a meeting, registering for events, acquiring a demo version, and completing a questionnaire. Conversely, e-mails are another story, and should be clear and specific; respondents will not waste time on reading them if they do not understand the general idea at first sight. Additionally, some people are used to reading in a diagonal or upward manner, which may complicate matters.

Generally, lead generation copywriting – like everything else in lead generation – requires more skill, than artistic license. No offense meant here! It is possible to learn how to create good lead generation text over time. However, it requires consistent education by studying the best copywriters' experience, daily practices, and of course, testing. The best lessons are gained through monitoring the results of different texts, through which copywriters are able to achieve maximum efficiency for sales growth.

Contact List Managers

Pay special attention to contact list managers, who are instrumental in **gathering information about your suspects and prospects, enlarging, structuring, segmentation, and updating**. Key requirements for these managers are almost opposite from what we want to see in successful telemarketing staff.

First of all, psychologically speaking, they are typically introverts who can work with **large amounts of data** for extended periods of time, and are often advanced computer users. For example, our contact list managers have masterfully used MS Office basic features, have had experience in CRM management, e-mail marketing, and internal software for contact list management. By using these tools, they have compared lists of contacts through set criteria, deleted double contacts, merged lists, broken text into cells which can be transposed, edited registries, and many other small miracles.

It is important that contact lists managers should be able to deal well with IT people who are responsible for CRM or other repositories where contact information is stored. They should be able to work alongside the support center of your cloud provider. It's not that they need to be techies themselves – it's about the correct diagnosis of a problem. Programmers can usually do just about anything your business requires (if your desires do not contradict each other!) A contact list manager should have a working knowledge of what kinds of data can be optimized with the assistance of programmers, and initiate direction of technical tasks.

Contact list managers working in our team have also been responsible for the creation of new lists. They have searched for new sources, estimated event lists, and subcontractors who may have already been solicited. Sometimes, they have coordinated a team of freelancers to format and segment data. In general, this type of work is "invisible," but very important for enabling further lead generation.

In conclusion, **the control of lead generation is an important factor** of its success. Here is a humorous illustration of what I mean:
- How many people work here?
- Ten, including a foreman.
- And without a foreman?
- Without a foreman, no one is working!

Without quality leadership, a team can quickly become confused and unproductive as people may lose interest and become lazy. Therefore, a lead generation director (or any other person executing this role) must be aware of the current state of affairs with lead generation campaigns and ensure that no one is lax with their duties.

Stick-and-Carrot Tactic for Lead Generation Managers

Usually, people with high career potential do not stay for a long time in telemarketing or contact list work. If they feel they are constrained professionally and forced into frameworks, they are more likely to leave for greener pastures. Copywriters need to be inspired about their work, since everyone wants to have a **potential to grow and develop their abilities.**

A lead generation director or CEO should understand the essence of this type of work, which is based partly on statistics, and partly on psychology. It is important to create the proper emotional and intellectual backgrounds for these processes. **Employees should be aware of the importance of their work**, and recognize that it is they who are responsible for its overall quality – after all, it is exactly like this!

In this regard, one needs to devise a transparent and attractive system of financial motivation. To quote John D. Rockefeller: "The ability to deal with people is as purchasable a commodity as sugar or coffee, and I will pay more for that ability than for any other under the sun." These words are perfectly applicable to lead generation as it requires a large number of communications. Thus, you should not skimp when allotting for positions which sales depend on. Good employees cost money and their salary should be, at the very least, the average wage level of a marketing manager. In addition, a lead generation warrior should be awarded with **bonuses for leads or prospects found**. It is fair to pay bonuses per lead (or suspect) because in further sales and closing processes, many other factors play a role; these factors include the actions of a sales team, pricing, and the competitive situation of the market. All of these things do not depend on lead quality and the lead generation manager's work. He or she has obtained or found a lead, and this work is done; for that, he or she should get a bonus (if the minimum requirements are met). At the same time, you may agree on an extra bonus for those leads that become sales, which makes the lead generation process even more inspiring.

In addition to bonuses, **team spirit** is very important for employees engaged in lead generation. To illustrate this, let us compare the lead generation process with fishing. It is well known that fishermen like to check what they have hooked and brag about successes, and lead generation is no different! Therefore, it is important to hold weekly meetings to share results, update status of leads, set common goals, and mark achievements. Here, it is essential to set a good pace for the game.

Outsourcing vs Hiring In-House
Leads to Take Away: Pros and Cons

Do we outsource or keep in-house? That is the question. Let me specify in advance that by outsourcing lead generation I mean **transferring the whole process to an outside supplier**. You set goals and in turn, you get leads. In this chapter, I shall not speak about any intermediate steps such as pay per click campaigns, landing generation, or outgoing calls without clear results. After all, they have no guarantee that you will reap any potential customers.

Actually, the decision of whether to outsource searching and attracting potential customers is **not a matter of cost**. Total expenses per employee are significantly higher for a company than just salaries, as this includes taxes, office space, a workstation, IT, holidays, sick-leaves, etc. As a result, the price of outsourcing is comparable to the cost of keeping your work in-house.

For many businesses, **establishing the lead generation process within a company is economically sound**. A definite advantage of this strategy is that expertise will be accumulated by your team. Company management also has full control over the situation. You can monitor and adjust employees' workloads in real-time. In addition, your own people will have a deeper understanding of the products you sell than any outside supplier.

Drawbacks of establishing a lead generation process within an enterprise are as follows. The company's management bears the risk of inaction or ineffectiveness of their employees. The employees may behave like this for a variety of reasons; an irrelevant marketing tool, problems with marketing pieces, an inaccurate target audience, low-skills, or banal laziness. Human factors add risks – an employee has a holiday or may retire – and the search for potential customers comes to a grinding halt.

The outsourcing of lead generation, above all, saves time and effort when organizing a staff's workload and its quality control. The implementation of new processes requires an expenditure of resources which may not always be available, and upon outsourcing this task, a company can focus on closing sales and will not be distracted by the added time and energy spent finding new potential customers and nurturing them.

However, there are **pitfalls**. First, the staff of an outsourcing agency has less institutional knowledge about your product line than your team does. Over time they will accumulate the necessary experience; however, this happens external of your company. Second, an outsourcing agency is likely to specialize in one method of lead generation such as online advertising or telemarketing. Therefore, your need to analyze results of one activity in comparison to another may not be realized. Third, you cannot monitor every employee working on a project as these employees are not your own. When considering whether to outsource such a workload or keep it in-house, you should evaluate the following pro and con arguments:

Model	Pros	Cons
Outsourcing	• saves time and effort on employee management and control; • no need to create a new business unit with its own processes; • no (or less) human dependency; • pay per result; • no overhead spent on office space and workstations; • an increased focus on closing sales.	• outsourcing agency's employees have less knowledge about your product than your experts; • you cannot monitor every employee; • inability to accumulate expertise on lead generation techniques; • the risk that your prospects may sooner or later be used for other projects.
Hiring In-House	• an accumulation of lead generation expertise and a thorough knowledge of offered products and services in comparison to an outside supplier; • full control over a situation; • deeper analysis of lead	• you are responsible for any ineffective work of your employees; • human factor risks (an employee may retire, or require sick days); • additional time and effort are required from company's marketing and

	generation tactics and flexibility in changing them; • ability to track and correct team's work at any time.	sales management; • need to control and motivate.

Types of Leads Providers

There are three main types of **lead generation providers**. Let me emphasize once again that I speak about pay per lead services where you get a lead as a final result; I am not discussing intermediate steps such as creating landings, adjusting a pay per click campaign, and conducting telemarketing. These groups mainly differ on how they attract leads; however, there are full-cycle agencies that include several services.

The first group includes companies looking for potential customers primarily **through telemarketing**. Some call centers provide these services on a pay per lead basis. While this is not true for all call centers, it is not uncommon for them to have a low staff qualification level, generally speaking. There is a problem of the professional outlook and overall erudition of the typical telemarketer. You can partially solve professional knowledge issues through the training, and subsequent testing of operators. Unfortunately, the second thing about overall erudition seems unable to be remedied. In most countries, telemarketing is a high stress, low-compensation job with a high staff turnover level. To fill the gaps left as a result of this turnover, call centers sometimes have to recruit personnel who lack the appropriate level of education and quality of speech to effectively communicate with even C-level management. They can speak only from a call script, which is rarely a good approach.

Sometimes, call center operators try to **speed up the process of making calls**; however, this practice can prove harmful to the quality level of the calls themselves. For example, upon receiving more or less a clear reply from a lead, a telemarketer will convert, and move on to the next call. This happens because their target can be set as high as 500 calls per day. Usually, call center employees are paid for conversations and per minute. Therefore, the best thing to do if you wish to work with a call center is to find one with background in your industry that functions on a pay per result basis.

Lead generation telemarketing agencies, as a rule, specialize in one or several key verticals. Therefore, their operators sound more professional when speaking to a target audience. In general, they possess more advanced communication skills and as such, take no issue with speaking to top managers and moving conversations along in the right direction. Practically all of them do not just call to reach their target audience, but also write personal e-mails and reminders, use business-oriented social networks, search for information on the web, and use a company's website contact forms to reach a prospective contact. They possess an arsenal of communication tools. They work by a pay per lead basis and a lead is usually "detected" through the arrangement of business meetings and conference calls, answering questionnaires, asking for proposal requests, and registration for an event. At the initial stage of cooperation, they usually run a test per labor hour to estimate the price per hot/warm and cold lead.

The most important thing to keep in mind when working with a call center or a telemarketing agency is to **agree on the target audience and the lead qualification criteria**. These are the basic parameters that will be used to look for leads. Here again, the quality and quantity need to be balanced; if you set the criteria too narrow, you will have fewer leads to start sales; too broad and you will get more leads, but some of them will not be ready for a purchasing process. Another item of note is that a lead generation agency can be rather hard to find. Sometimes, you even need to persuade them to take your project. As they become integrated into your sales and marketing processes, they can be very demanding when agreeing to work with customers. They work quietly, as partisans, and rarely do promotions. This is partly due to an inability to work simultaneously on competing products and the low scalability of this business.

The second large group of lead generation outsourcing suppliers is **internet agencies specializing in online advertising**. Some of them are willing to take responsibility for the result. They work on a pay per lead basis and the lead is either a contact form filled out on a landing or an incoming call. This type of lead generation service goes well for products that are widely searched for on the Internet. I can say that these agencies are also quite demanding in terms of choosing customers because they take responsibility for the number of leads provided. It is quite understandable – they cover the costs of an advertising campaign, its adjustments, the landing page, and its edits; they conduct tests to find the most effective version, and you get a lead as a result. Since compensation occurs on a pay per lead basis, a test project is completed to ensure that the cost is appropriate for services rendered. After the price per lead is determined, a final commercial proposal can be agreed upon.

However, there is another option. Some online lead generation agencies have a strict specialization in services such as credit, automotive, or insurance services. What they provide is a general landing page for acquiring leads for these services without any brand advertising and, furthermore, selling these leads to service providers. This is a fast way to get leads. A drawback of this approach is that it is not customizable, as no additional lead qualification criteria can be added to restrict or filter the outcome. This online business is more scalable than those described above, since it is limited to the number of target audience requests.

There is another option, however: **marketplaces and tendering websites, which help customers to find suppliers and vice versa**. "During the last few years at our company, we use more and more European marketplaces, which are web services that specialize in generating leads for businesses," says Benoit Bossuet, Lead Generation Manager for Neopost. "On one hand, they provide enterprises with highly competitive quotes from nationwide suppliers of office equipment and business services. On the other hand, these web services allow product and service suppliers to get new leads that are interested in certain categories of goods."

The main principle of marketplaces is as follows: people publish an announcement about the product or service they need and their requirements; suppliers send proposals and hope they will be chosen as subcontractors. **Marketplaces are the best venue for work that can be categorized, and buying of goods with clear specifications and simple commercial proposals**. This is because a supplier can create proposals quickly, and easily send out hundreds of them per day.

Tendering websites are more frequently **used for complicated purchases of services and consulting**, which has a more formalized purchase procedure. The average sum of a sale is significantly higher here. These sites are mostly used by enterprises, where every purchase will need to be run through a tender procedure to ensure a fair choice of a subcontractor for entities such as governmental bodies, or large public companies.

Freelance search websites are a kind of **marketplace for individual services**. They allow more flexibility and, consequently, bring more risks regarding quality and timeframe. Dealing with scammers is another risk, which has recently begun to decrease due to the active use of specialized secure payment systems. Still, scamming does happens, and without a contract you are never guaranteed the quality of work you will receive (if you receive it at all!). This being the case, freelancers are great options for small, not risky, and inexpensive work that can be completed entirely by an individual alone. However, when teamwork is required, it is better to sign a contract with a company that has a reliable reputation, a portfolio of successful projects, and a solid history.

In marketplaces and tendering websites, **leads are mostly qualified in terms of having an interest, a need, a determined timeframe for making a purchase**, and some budget. However, additional lead criteria that are applicable to your lead generation campaign and sales process may disqualify a lead altogether.

These services work when there is a **certain demand**. People should realize that they have a need and announce it. You cannot influence this process if have an innovative product. Moreover, marketplaces and tendering websites do not work when a customer prefers and is able to choose a subcontractor through **live communication** (such as at an event, or via telemarketing). The customer may also just choose from vendors **not listed in a marketplace** by some other criteria, such as a rating of companies. Also, marketplaces are often **regionally-specific;** that is to say, you can order practically everything you need for your project in some Asian marketplaces, while in another part of the world (Australia, perhaps), marketplaces supply only a few categories of goods and products.

The lead generation sphere is quite interesting in terms of new ideas; periodically, new businesses appear and well-known companies enlarge their services. Google has been testing the pay per lead model since at least 2011, but there has not been a release with which to quantify their results. I think this is due to an individual approach being needed for every product and every competitive environment. For now, Google offers a **pay per acquisition** service as part of their traffic optimization services. It enables a Google-engineered algorithm to display your ad to an audience that is more likely to take some action. You can still pay per click, but your bids are set up in such a way as to acquire more conversions.

Many lead generation start-ups appear every year; however, in most cases, they disappear just as quickly. Classic, proven approaches such as telemarketing and pay per click advertising in conjunction with a landing page still dominate the market.

How much does a lead cost when outsourced?

It is up to a company to understand the optimal cost per lead that they can afford to pay, and to find a subcontractor able to provide qualified leads for the best price. However, 26% of Lead Generation

Benchmark Report respondents surveyed say that they do not know what the maximum cost is they are willing to pay for a lead.

The **cost of a lead is determined by the efforts that agencies spend on its detection**. Therefore, the first stage of collaboration is a test project, which serves to discover how many qualified leads occur in an average sample of the target audience. Then, upon justification of the lead's cost, the pay per result work can begin. Some agencies also receive awards when leads turn into sales, such as a percentage from contract/profit, or a fixed amount.

As a result, the cost of a lead is influenced by different things. Such influences are the **cost of specialists per hour, direct expenses for a campaign (like clicks or calls), and marketing materials related to a project**. In addition, there are also external factors that depend on a product, including the **product's characteristics and its price compared to competitors, the size of a target audience, the market situation, and the company's brand**. As a result, the cost of a lead varies from a **few pennies to thousands of dollars.**

For example, the price for a person that subscribes to a business trainer's newsletter may start at as low as several cents. A lead for a large scale ERP project may cost as high as thousands of dollars. The high price of a lead is justified if these leads bring big sales. If it were possible to predict a lead with a 100% conversion rate to a sale, many companies would be eager to pay even more for it.

Final Remarks
What if lead generation "does not work?"

Using the techniques described in this book, you can significantly increase the number of leads. The results you may get depend on the specifics of your products, their target audience, the competitive environment, and further sales work. If lead generation is still "not working," please check if the following rules are observed:

- **Appropriate methods.** Each company needs to experiment with and utilize a diverse array of marketing tools to develop its promotional strategy and plan. Perhaps some other tool will work more efficiently for your product; for example, if trying to arrange business meetings has the unwanted side effect of your head smashing into more desk tops or brick walls than usual, try inviting your targeted attendees to a seminar. Having exhausted the efficiency of purchasing contact lists, utilize social networks to explore new opportunities.

- **A sufficient number of calls per day.** If an employee makes at least 100 calls to an appropriate target audience, results are inevitable. It is desirable that your telemarketers see how many calls they make. This can be automated by using IP telephony or call center software. If you do not have these options, at least ask telemarketers to put a "tick" near a list of numbers from 1 to 100. If only a small number of calls are completed, then it is no wonder that there are no leads; lead generation is all about statistics! The daily target number for calls can be higher than 100, but you need to understand that with such a high volume, it is more difficult to treat each call individually and give prospective buyers the time and attention needed to answer their questions or concerns. For comparison, the daily target of call centers is approximately 500 calls. However, this affects the quality of call conversation, and does not afford telemarketing agents the time to properly prepare for every call.

- **Up-to-date and detailed marketing lists**. These lists should correspond to your target audience and contain detailed segmentation. Over time, even the best lists become exhausted. In this case, you can use the previously described methods of expanding of your contacts; whether on your own, working with call centers, or purchasing such lists from contact data providers. Please note that newly purchased lists should not overlap with those you have compiled so far – it is a matter of integrating CRM with an online data service provider, or lots of manual work.

- **Excellent selling texts and marketing pieces**. It's disappointing to set up the entire lead generation workflow and to fail due to the text you create. Try to send texts out for testing, consult with colleagues of the same industry, and finally ask your customers about what works best. It is important to get feedback and take it into account when finalizing marketing pieces. If possible, try to attract your sales department and staff who work directly with customers (be it in production, or support) to help you determine what can be improved with the text.

- **Online demand.** Before launching any online lead generation campaign, make sure there is sufficient demand for your product or service on the Net. Otherwise, if you propose a new category of goods, you should be prepared for the fact that your campaign should create brand awareness prior to proceeding.

- **Online advertising.** Do people search for your category of goods but do not click your ads? Or maybe your ads aren't displaying at all? Okay, let's fix that. The most common reason regarding why ads are not coming up in search results is a lack of advertising budget. Try to narrow your target group (for example, by region) and choose more specific search keywords. For example, do not use "marketing conference" – instead, use "marketing conference Los Angeles." If the ads are being shown but people do not click on them, the problem can be narrowed down to the text. Make your text as close to the search request as possible, and have it be as attractive as you can both sonically, and aesthetically.

- **Landings.** If there is a steady demand, you are sure about the competitiveness of the product in comparison to other providers, and people search the relevant keywords and click on your ad but your visitors do not convert into leads, the evident problem is in the landing. Please check that you have done enough testing, creating different versions of headings and call-to-actions, and are following our recommendations regarding successful landing setups.

- **Lead criteria problems**. Sometimes, a telemarketer or an online advertising specialist wants to get more leads so much that they start persuading the sales department that the lead criteria are too narrow and they cannot follow them. This results in creating more leads which will unfortunately dead-end. The director of lead generation or the marketing director should prevent such situations and help craft an optimum balance. Both parties should understand that the strictness of lead criteria influences their quantity (and cost), and develop a good lead nurturing program for cold leads.

- **Sales work**. Sometimes, it happens that the leads are good, but the sales conversion rate is low. This may also be due to a low level of sales. Try to analyze the situation and trace all steps of your sales managers when dealing with leads and closing sales. Listen to phone conversations and attend pertinent meetings. It makes sense to seek outside help to assess the effectiveness of your team's work; this will help to close the maximum number of deals, and thus increase the conversion rate.

- **A common understanding of the lead generation process by all participants** (lead generation, marketing, sales, call center, outsourcing agency). Rifts in business processes can be discussed and argued about by employees for ages. The truth is important; however, a single position is more important. The head of a company/department must at some point stop debates and apply a clear interpretation to all parties.

Conclusion

Lead generation is **necessary for all businesses that do active sales and need an increase in their sales volume**. It is lead generation that provides easily measurable indicators of effectiveness through the sales conversion rate – a percentage of potential customers turning into actual sales. Having implemented and adjusted the lead generation workflow, a company's management understands what the **cost of a potential customer** is and how much effort has to be invested to find a lead and to close a sale. This helps companies **eliminate the risk that they will "run out" of potential clients**, enables them to feel **independent from incidents that occur from sales and human factors**, and prevents wasting **a marketing budget on ineffective activities**.

Thank you for your attention! I hope that you have found this book useful and it has served as a foundation for building your lead generation strategy, or helped improve the effectiveness of your workflow by delivering new prospective customers, cultivating sales, and ultimately, increasing profits.

Please feel free to write me and share your thoughts and experiences with lead generation: ksenia.andreeva2007@gmail.com.

I would also greatly appreciate your feedback about my book at Amazon.com.

ABOUT THE AUTHOR

Ksenia Andreeva is an international expert on lead generation. She has over 11 years of practice with lead generation, sales, marketing, PR and event management. She is the founder and the owner of NWComm, a lead generation agency. In her book, written in a simple manner with lots of practical examples, case studies, business jokes, and current statistics, Ksenia describes the main lead generation terms, key formulas, and most popular methodology.

1

Made in the USA
Coppell, TX
02 March 2021